W9-AZL-544

LEE BAILEY'S
Dinners at Home

LEE BAILEY'S
Dinners at Home

BY LEE BAILEY

PHOTOGRAPHS BY TOM ECKERLE

CLARKSON POTTER/PUBLISHERS
NEW YORK

Copyright © 1995 by Lee Bailey
Photographs copyright © 1995 by Tom Eckerle

All rights reserved. No part of this book may be reproduced or transmitted in any form or by any means, electronic or mechanical, including photocopying, recording, or by any information storage and retrieval system, without permission in writing from the publisher.

Published by Clarkson N. Potter, Inc., 201 East 50th Street, New York, New York 10022. Member of the Crown Publishing Group.

Random House, Inc. New York, Toronto, London, Sydney, Auckland

CLARKSON N. POTTER, POTTER, and colophon are trademarks of Clarkson N. Potter, Inc.

Manufactured in China

Design by Donna Agajanian

Library of Congress Cataloging-in-Publication Data
Bailey, Lee.
     Lee Bailey's dinners at home / by Lee Bailey ; photographs by Tom
Eckerle. — 1st ed.
        p.   cm.
     Includes index.
     1. Dinners and dining.   2. Entertaining.   3. Menus.   I. Title.
     II. Title: Dinners at home.
     TX737.B35   1995
     642'.4—dc20
                                                              95-3184
                                                                CIP

ISBN 0-517-59245-2

10   9   8   7   6   5   4   3   2   1

First Edition

Thanks to Tom Eckerle and his assistant, Barry Kornbluh.

For their help in the kitchen, thank you to James Lartin, Erica Wood, Nola Chaffee, Joseph Obermayer, Sean Lousfjed, and Kendle Pettigrove.

For offering locations for the photographs, thanks to Pam Bernstein and George Friedman, Ina and Jeffrey Garten, Tom Booth, Peri Wolfman and Charley Gold, and Lee Mindel.

For their cooperation in providing table settings, thanks go to Nikki Gannon and Loren Pack at ABC Carpet & Home; Mark Lewis at Ad Hoc Softwares; Joel Dean, Jim Mellgren, and Reba Hassett at Dean & DeLuca; Barbara Eigen Arts; Linda Saltzman at Sasaki; Linda Sylvester and Carl Peterson at Sylvester & Co.; Michael McDavitt and James Griffin at Takashimaya; Larry Kiss at Williams-Sonoma; and Lois Granger and Sharron Lewis at Wolfman·Gold & Good Company.

ACKNOWLEDGMENTS

CONTENTS

I know there are plenty of ways to enjoy friends, but when you get right down to it, I'm convinced the best way is with a dinner at home—and I'm more than a little dismayed and puzzled at how apprehensive or reluctant so many people are about this. When I was growing up my father—who always cooked for his pals and their families—clearly got so much pure and simple enjoyment from getting together with them. Could it be that those of us who write about food and entertaining have presented the subject in such a way that, instead of encouraging folks to get into the kitchen and whip up a meal to be shared, we've made it seem more a chore than the pleasure it should be? I hope not.

Look, I know everyone is busy these days, but does that have to preclude the kind of comforting rewards we get from the company of those beyond our immediate families whom we care about seeing? I repeat, I feel the best, most relaxing place to do this is in the home. So, plan a little dinner party.

I want to help you make it happen. With this objective in mind, and using what I've gathered from conversations with people from all over the country, I decided to take nine of my favorite meals and make them as near to foolproof as possible. I hope this will provide you with an expandable portfolio of ideas to work from, which will not only erase your resistance to entertaining, but will also encourage you to take advantage of the genuine joy of sharing a meal with a group of friends.

Let me explain what I mean by an "expandable" portfolio. I've given you complete menus here for meals I particularly like, and I've given you a way to approach them in the time plans. But with each I've also added a second menu based on a new main dish. What this should do—besides offering a second option for a chicken dinner or a casserole supper—is give you an idea of how

INTROD

to pull together your own menus from the recipes in the book and tailor them to specific occasions, individual preferences, and time limitations.

I think there's a little something for everyone here—meals that can be slowly cooked while you are at home for the day puttering around or catching up (on your rest or closet cleaning), suppers you can put together on short notice, casserole dinners you can prepare in advance, and heaps more.

Before we start, I want to give you a few little tips. Keep in mind that you should do your best to make the evening relaxing. So, my advice is, don't try to be too much of a perfectionist. For instance, you don't have to cook every dessert you serve. We all know there are wonderful ice creams, sherbets, cookies, and such available. There are frozen piecrusts just waiting to be filled. Take advantage of these convenient alternatives if you are pressed for time or if you don't particularly like to make desserts. The same is true with breads and rolls. There's a glorious selection out there in specialty shops.

Aside from frozen piecrusts, there are frozen, canned, and powdered stocks. And while it's almost as simple to make some concoctions—like salad dressing—from scratch, don't do it if you find a commercial brand that tastes right to you. You're the judge.

I do have to draw the line someplace, however. I haven't gone so far as to suggest the cream-of-mushroom-soup-in-the-casserole routine here. But if you find ways to make shortcuts work for you and you're satisfied with the results, what your guests don't know won't hurt them.

So, remember, be subjective, be cool, stick to foods and menus that make sense to you—and that you like—and keep in mind that the important thing is to have the party.

Eat, drink, and be merry—I promise you'll be glad you did.

UCTION

BEEF DINN

he beef being served nowadays is different from what was popular only a decade ago. Today the public seems more attracted to leaner cuts, which have all the old familiar flavor without the old familiar fat and calories. Gone are the days of heavily marbled roasts and steaks. And I say good riddance. Now even traditional dishes like classic boiled beef are generally well trimmed before serving.

The two party menus I have devised are built around that classic boiled beef and a superlean tenderloin of beef. The boiled beef is topped with a tasty horseradish sauce; for the tenderloin, I've perked up the sauce with green peppercorns. You can make the dishes less calorie-intensive by substituting a prepared salsa for the sauces, or just serve the beef in the English manner, simply accompanied by a bit of grainy mustard and a few sour pickles. Both menus utilize the same accompaniment, potatoes and cauliflower cooked in milk to make them more creamy, then mashed with roasted garlic.

The next course is a salad made of simple mixed greens (in any combination that suits your fancy), accompanied by a wedge of your favorite cheese. The dessert is a refreshing citrus-flavored crumble with the added surprise of banana whipped cream.

All easy and festive—and designed to serve six.

ERS

Menu I

Boiled Brisket of Beef
(page 12)

Horseradish Sauce
(page 14)

Potatoes Mashed with Cauliflower
(page 17)

Mixed Salad
(page 17)

Cheese

Crusty Rolls

Tropical Crumble
(page 18)

Banana Whipped Cream
(page 18)

PRECEDING PAGES: **The table has been set with a mix of old and new pieces.** BELOW: **The water should barely cover the meat.** BELOW RIGHT: **Slice the brisket in medium-thick slices.** OPPOSITE: **Both the meat and potatoes have been topped with a bit of the sauce.**

Boiled Brisket of Beef

This dish has been a favorite of mine for years. Try it and you'll see why.

1 6-pound brisket of beef
2 medium onions, peeled
2 unpeeled carrots, scrubbed and broken into several pieces
1 tablespoon coarse salt
4 celery ribs, washed and broken into several pieces
2 bay leaves
4 parsley stems
Several sprigs of thyme (or 1 teaspoon dried thyme)

Put the meat in a Dutch oven or other deep pot with a lid and barely cover with water. Add all the other ingredients (see the photograph below). Bring quickly to a boil over high heat. Turn back to a simmer (the surface of the water should barely bubble) and cook, covered, until fork-tender, 3 to 4 hours. Check it periodically and use a slotted spoon to skim off any of the scum that rises to the surface. Add more boiling water as needed. Leave the meat in the cooking liquid until you're ready to serve it.

To serve, remove the beef from the cooking liquid and slice it across the grain (see the photograph below).

Serves 6 (with leftovers)

Cook the brisket a day ahead. Allow it to cool in the cooking liquid, then slice it across the grain. Put the slices back into the cooking liquid and store, covered, in the refrigerator. To serve, remove any fat that has congealed on the surface and allow the meat to come to room temperature. Warm it in the liquid over medium heat until hot, 10 to 15 minutes.

Prepare the crumble. Bake it now, and if you plan to serve it warm, simply reheat briefly before serving.

Whip the heavy cream and store it in a metal strainer set over a bowl in the refrigerator; a small amount of moisture will separate from it. When you are ready to serve, discard the liquid and mash the banana in the bowl. Stir in the vanilla and beat in the cream.

Make the vinaigrette. Assemble the salad on individual plates (undressed) and put them back into the refrigerator. Take the cheese out ahead of time to come to room temperature.

Put the potatoes and garlic into the oven to bake. While they are baking, separate the cauliflower florets and put them on to cook. Once the potatoes and garlic are cooked, finish them and set aside. If you keep them at room temperature, they will take only 15 minutes or so to reheat.

Make the horseradish sauce. Keep it warm until you are ready to serve.

Horseradish Sauce

The important thing in this recipe is to be sure the onions are lightly browned. This adds considerably to the sauce's flavor. I also usually use considerably more than the ¼ cup of horseradish called for here, but let your taste be your guide.

4 tablespoons (½ stick) unsalted butter (or half butter and half margarine)
½ cup minced onion
3 tablespoons all-purpose flour
2 cups rich chicken stock, heated
1 tablespoon fresh lemon juice
¼ teaspoon pepper
¼ cup prepared horseradish (or more, to taste)
Salt (optional)

Melt the butter in a large skillet. Add the onion and cook over medium-high heat until golden, about 5 minutes. Sprinkle in the flour and cook, stirring, for a minute or so. Stir in the hot stock, mixing as you go to eliminate any lumps. Stir in the lemon juice and pepper. Reduce the heat to low and simmer, stirring occasionally, until the sauce thickens, about 10 minutes. Stir in the horseradish. Add a little salt if necessary.

You can allow this to cool and reheat it.

Makes about 2 cups

VARIATION

Horseradish and Green Peppercorn Sauce

Prepare the recipe as above. When you stir in the horseradish, add 1 tablespoon Dijon mustard and 2 tablespoons drained, brine-packed green peppercorns.

Stir the mustard and green peppercorns into the sauce for the variation.

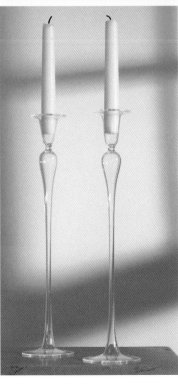

Setting the Table

Antique damask, silver, crystal, and china have been used on this table setting. The china is a period 1920s pattern from Tiffany & Co. The dinner fork and knife are the Christofle "Albi" pattern; the salad fork is related, but unmatched. The crystal is "Paris" from Baccarat. Wild asters, feverfew, and yellow poppies in an old, creamware urn round out the color scheme, and the old glass candlesticks add a bit of sparkle and height to the arrangement.

TOP: Mashing the potatoes and cauliflower with a hand masher keeps the mixture light. ABOVE: We used a mix of red leaf lettuce, Boston lettuce, and radicchio for the salad.

Potatoes Mashed with Cauliflower

Of course, you can boil the potatoes for this, but I bake them. Then I butter and salt the scooped-out skins, and toast them to use as an hors d'oeuvre.

    3 pounds baking potatoes
    3 tablespoons olive oil
    1 large head of garlic
    2 generous cups cauliflower florets and tender stems
    Low-fat milk
    6 tablespoons (¾ stick) unsalted butter (or butter substitute)
    1½ teaspoons salt or to taste
    Black pepper to taste

Preheat the oven to 350 degrees.

Rub the potatoes with 2 tablespoons of the olive oil and bake until tender, about 1 hour. At the same time, slice about ½ inch off the top of the garlic to expose the cloves. Rub the head with the remaining 1 tablespoon oil, wrap it in aluminum foil, and put it in to roast with the potatoes for 30 minutes. Set aside; leave the oven on.

In a large saucepan (use a 4-quart pan so it won't boil over), cover the cauliflower with low-fat milk and bring to a boil. Turn back to a slow boil and cook until just tender, about 10 minutes. Drain the cauliflower, reserving the milk.

Scoop out the hot potato pulp into a large warm bowl. Squeeze the garlic pulp into the potatoes—use as much or as little as you like. Add the butter and mash with an old-fashioned hand masher (do not use an electric mixer, as it will make the mixture glutinous). Add the cauliflower and mash with the potatoes, adding about ¾ cup of the cauliflower milk. Salt and pepper to taste.

Butter a 2-quart heatproof casserole and scrape the mixture into it. Smooth the top with a spatula and rub it with a bit of butter. Bake, uncovered, for 5 to 10 minutes, until hot.

    Serves 6

Mixed Salad

Use any combination of greens for this. Accompany it with your favorite cheese, at room temperature. We used Asiago for the photograph.

VINAIGRETTE

    6 tablespoons olive oil
    2 tablespoons red wine vinegar
    2 teaspoons Dijon mustard
    Salt and pepper to taste

    8 cups mixed salad greens, washed and dried

Whisk together the ingredients for the vinaigrette. Assemble the greens on individual plates and drizzle with the vinaigrette.

    Serves 6

Tropical Crumble

This makes a refreshing finish to any meal—with or without the whipped cream.

½ large pineapple, peeled, cored, and cut into ½-inch cubes
4 large seedless oranges, peeled (with white pith cut off) and sectioned
3 tablespoons fresh lemon juice
1 cup shredded unsweetened coconut
¾ cup granulated sugar
1 cup all-purpose flour
½ cup packed light brown sugar
8 tablespoons (1 stick) unsalted butter, softened

Preheat the oven to 350 degrees.

Generously butter an 8-inch square or oval pan or baking dish. Toss the pineapple and oranges with the lemon juice and half of the coconut. Heap into the buttered dish. Sprinkle ¼ cup of the granulated sugar over all.

Mix together the remaining coconut with the remaining ½ cup granulated sugar. Add the flour and brown sugar and use your fingers to rub in the butter until the mixture is crumbly. Pat onto the fruit.

Bake until the top begins to turn golden, about 45 minutes.

Serve with Banana Whipped Cream or vanilla ice cream.

Serves 6

Banana Whipped Cream

This whipped cream has many uses—try it on everything from fresh fruit to custards and cakes.

1 cup heavy cream
1 tablespoon sugar
½ teaspoon vanilla extract (or bourbon)
1 ripe medium banana, mashed

In a chilled bowl, whip the cream and sugar until it almost stands in soft peaks. Add the vanilla and banana. Beat to blend.

Makes about 1½ cups

TOP: Pat the crumble mixture gently and evenly over the fruit. ABOVE: Serve the crumble in a deep plate with a generous spoonful of the Banana Whipped Cream.

Baked Tenderloin of Beef

As you probably know, this is an expensive cut of meat. However, it's quick and easy to cook and there is no fat or waste.

1 beef tenderloin (3¾ pounds trimmed weight)
Salt and black pepper to taste
Canola oil

Preheat the oven to 400 degrees.

Rub the beef all over with salt and pepper. Rub a heavy ovenproof skillet with a little canola oil and brown the meat on all sides over high heat, about 8 minutes. Use tongs—not a fork—to turn the meat as you brown it. (Cut the beef into 2 equal halves if necessary to fit it into your skillet.)

Place the browned tenderloin—still in the skillet—in the oven and bake until the internal temperature is 120 degrees, 25 to 30 minutes. Remove to a cutting board and cover with a tent of foil. Allow to rest for 10 minutes before slicing.

Serve slices topped with some of the Horseradish and Green Peppercorn Sauce.

NOTE: The beef will continue to cook a little while it is resting. It's very important not to overcook this cut of beef. Usually when you buy a tenderloin, one end is thicker than the other. Always test the thickest part for doneness. Obviously the thinner part will be more well-done for those who prefer it that way.

Serves 6 to 8

RIGHT: For the best flavor, make sure to brown the tenderloin on all sides. Turn it with tongs rather than a fork so you don't lose any of the juices. OPPOSITE: The sauce shouldn't cover the meat entirely.

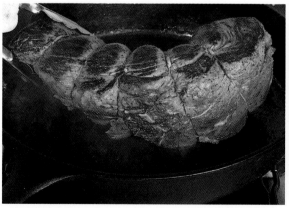

CASSEROLE

I confess that I have a problem with what was once considered the "classic" casserole dinner. Too often it conjures up something where you open several cans—one of which is usually cream of mushroom soup—mix them all together, top with grated cheese, and bake in a 375-degree oven until bubbly and browned on top. Of course, this is only one type of casserole. Lumping everything under this limited description would mean missing out on a whole range of nourishing, easy-to-prepare—not to mention crowd-pleasing—dishes. And nine times out of ten they can be prepared in advance.

Most casserole dinners need nothing more than a salad and dessert to round them out, but here I've added a few more elements (which you can leave out if you want to keep things simple).

The first menu starts with a corn and pepper soup and includes such flourishes as tortilla puffs and a jam cake for dessert. Now the casserole itself with a salad would be enough, but the puffs and jam cake could certainly be made ahead and set aside.

The second menu illustrates just how simple, uncomplicated, and flexible casserole dinners can be. Here again, you can add to it to make it a formal and more important meal. And like the previous one it can be changed with the addition of another course or two—still prepared in advance so the most you will have to do at mealtime is heat the casserole and toss the salad.

These casseroles serve a crowd, so I've written the menus for eight.

DINNERS

Creamed Corn and Red Bell Pepper Soup

This delightful soup freezes quite well. For that reason, I always make a double batch and freeze individual portions.

2 tablespoons unsalted butter
2 cups thinly sliced leeks, white parts only (3 or 4 medium leeks)
1 cup thinly sliced shallots
6 cups rich chicken stock (low-salt canned may be substituted)
1 baking potato, peeled and diced
½ cup diced red bell pepper
3 cups fresh or frozen yellow corn kernels
1½ teaspoons salt (or less, depending on how salty the stock is)
½ teaspoon white pepper

OPTIONAL GARNISHES
Crème fraîche or plain yogurt
Snipped chives

Melt the butter over medium heat in a heavy medium saucepan with a tight-fitting lid. Add the leeks and shallots and toss in the butter; cover with the lid. Reduce the heat to very low and sweat the vegetables, stirring several times, until wilted but not browned, about 15 minutes.

Stir in the stock and bring quickly to a boil over high heat. Then turn back to a simmer. Add the potato and bell pepper. Cover and simmer for 15 minutes. Add the corn and bring to a simmer. Cover and cook for 5 minutes.

Puree the soup mixture in a food processor or blender. Push through a sieve; discard the solids. Taste the strained puree for salt and pepper. Serve warm or chilled, garnished with a few dollops of crème fraîche or yogurt and sprinkled with some snipped chives if you like.

Serves 8

PRECEDING PAGES: **The main course from Menu I—rather than making a separate course, we served the salad on the plate with the casserole.**

TOP: The soup is garnished with a dollop of crème fraîche and a sprinkling of snipped chives. ABOVE LEFT: Stir in the corn and bring the soup back to a simmer. ABOVE AND LEFT: After the soup has been pureed, use the back of a ladle or spoon to push it through a fine sieve.

Turkey and Cheese Enchilada Casserole

This is guaranteed to be a crowd pleaser.

TURKEY

    1 4½-pound whole turkey breast, with the bone in

    1 teaspoon salt

    1 teaspoon pepper

TOMATO SAUCE

    ½ cup olive oil

    4 ½ cups roughly chopped onions

    2 generous tablespoons roughly chopped garlic

    4 28-ounce cans whole peeled tomatoes (without paste), drained

    1 teaspoon salt

    1 teaspoon black pepper

    1 teaspoon dried oregano

    2 teaspoons dried basil

    6 tablespoons hot chili powder

CARAMELIZED ONIONS

    3 medium onions, roughly chopped (see Note on page 45)

ASSEMBLY

    Vegetable oil

    10 flour tortillas

    1 pound cheddar cheese, shredded

    1 pound Monterey jack cheese, shredded

Preheat the oven to 350 degrees.

    Make the turkey. Rub the breast inside and out with the salt and pepper.

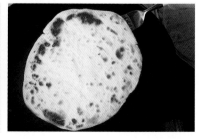

Place on a rack in a roasting pan and roast until the internal temperature reaches 160 degrees, about 1 hour and 20 minutes.

Set the turkey aside to cool. When cool enough to handle, remove the skin and shred the meat. Measure out 3⅓ cups and reserve. Use any leftover turkey meat for another purpose.

Make the tomato sauce. Heat the oil in a very large deep sauté pan over medium-high heat. Add the onions and cook until wilted, about 5 minutes. Add the garlic and cook for another minute. Stir in the tomatoes, salt, pepper, and herbs until combined. Gently crush the tomatoes with the back of a wooden spoon to release their juices (see photograph below left); bring the sauce to a boil. Turn the heat back to a simmer and cook, uncovered, until reduced and thickened, 25 to 30 minutes. Let the sauce cool for a minute or two, then pass it through the coarse die of a food mill.

Measure out 5 cups of sauce and reserve. If you have much more, return the sauce to the skillet and reduce it to about 5 cups. Stir in the chili powder.

Make the caramelized onions. Place a large cast-iron skillet over high heat. When very hot, add one-third of the onions. Allow to cook without stirring for 4 to 5 minutes, until they get brown. Use a spatula to turn them over and brown the other side, about another 4 minutes. (See the photograph on page 45.) Carefully wipe out the skillet and repeat with the other batches of onions.

Assemble the casserole. Preheat the oven to 350 degrees.

Lightly oil a cast-iron skillet and set over high heat. Soften the tortillas by cooking them for about 30 seconds on each side.

Mix the 2 cheeses together in a bowl. Spread about ⅓ cup of the sauce over the bottom of an 11 × 9-inch casserole dish (you can use a foil one).

Place the tortillas on the countertop and fill each with ¼ cup sauce, 2 tablespoons caramelized onions, ¼ cup of the mixed cheeses, and ⅓ cup shredded turkey meat. Roll the tortillas around the filling (see the photograph below). Place the rolled enchiladas, seam side down, in a single layer in the prepared dish. Cover with the remaining sauce and sprinkle with the remaining cheeses. Bake until bubbly and very lightly browned on top, 40 to 45 minutes.

Serves 8 generously

NOTE: It's important that you chop these onions by hand instead of in the food processor. The food processor releases too much liquid from the onions for this cooking method.

ABOVE LEFT: Use a fork and a spoon to serve the casserole. FROM FAR LEFT: Crushing the tomatoes helps release their juices. Use a food mill to puree. The tortillas will brown when you heat them in the skillet. Wrap the tortilla around the filling. Sprinkle the casserole evenly with cheese.

TOP: You can grate the carrots directly into the mixing bowl, using the large holes on a four-sided grater. ABOVE: The Puffed Tortilla Triangles would make a fine appetizer with your favorite dip.

Puffed Tortilla Triangles

These are so popular that you might want to double or even triple this recipe.

Safflower or canola oil
8 to 10 flour tortillas, each cut into 4 triangles
Coarse salt to taste

Place an omelet pan over medium-high heat. Pour about ¼ inch of oil in the pan. When hot (the oil should be shimmering), add 4 tortilla triangles and fry, turning once, until puffy and golden on each side, about 30 seconds per side. Drain and sprinkle with salt. Repeat until all are done.

Serves 8

Endive and Carrot Salad with Raspberry Vinaigrette

The flavor of raspberry vinaigrette is a perfect companion to any combination of greens—especially those that are slightly bitter or peppery.

7 large heads of Belgian endive, cut crosswise into ½-inch pieces
2 carrots, scraped and grated
1 teaspoon salt
½ teaspoon black pepper
2 tablespoons raspberry vinegar
6 tablespoons canola oil
3 tablespoons olive oil
¼ cup fresh raspberries

Toss together the endive and carrots in a large bowl. In a separate bowl or a large measuring cup, mix the salt, pepper, and vinegar. Gradually whisk in the oils. Mash the berries into the vinaigrette with a fork.

Toss the salad with the vinaigrette and place on individual plates. Top each serving with a grind of pepper if you like.

Serves 8

Mash the berries directly into the vinaigrette with a fork.

Time Plan

Virtually every part of this menu can be completed ahead of time. All that has to be done at the last minute is reheating the casserole and assembling the salad—and reheating the soup.

Start by roasting the turkey breast, and while it is in the oven, make the tomato sauce. With the sauce simmering, caramelize the onions for the casserole and set them aside. When the turkey is cooked, allow it to cool and then shred the meat. Next, assemble the casserole. It is easier to bake the casserole ahead of time and then reheat it when you are ready to serve it. If it is kept at room temperature, reheating should take 20 or 30 minutes in a moderate oven.

Once the casserole is prepared, make the soup and puree it.

Next, start the cake. While the cake is in the oven, whip the cream and store it in a metal strainer over a bowl in the refrigerator. When the cake is cool, assemble it and set it aside until is is ready to be served.

Now fry the Tortilla Triangles. (They can be done in advance if you have more time to do them earlier than now.)

The last thing to work on is the salad. Wash and spin dry the greens (they can be done in advance and wrapped in a towel in the refrigerator). Shake together the vinaigrette and dress the salad just before serving it.

Almond-Blackberry Jam Cake

Almonds are my favorite in this cake, but obviously any other nut can be substituted. Use the best jam you can find.

1 cup slivered almonds, toasted
1¾ cups sifted all-purpose flour
¼ teaspoon baking soda
8 tablespoons (1 stick) unsalted butter, softened
1½ cups sugar
3 large eggs, separated
⅔ cup sour cream
1 teaspoon vanilla extract
1 to 1½ cups blackberry jam

OPTIONAL GARNISH

Lightly whipped cream spiked with a few tablespoons of flavored brandy (blackberry, if it is handy)

Preheat the oven to 325 degrees. Grease and lightly flour two 8-inch round cake pans.

Coarsely chop the toasted almonds and set aside. In a large bowl, sift the flour with the baking soda. Set aside a few tablespoons of the flour mixture on a plate.

In a medium bowl, cream the butter with the sugar with an electric mixer until light and fluffy, about 3 minutes. Add the egg yolks, one at a time, beating well after each addition.

Stir the dry ingredients into the egg and butter mixture alternately with the sour cream, beginning and ending with the flour. Stir in the vanilla and mix well.

Lightly dredge the almonds in the reserved flour on the plate, shaking off any excess. Stir into the batter.

In a very clean medium bowl (copper, if you have one), beat the egg whites until stiff peaks form. Gently stir one-third of the whites into the batter to soften it; fold in the remaining whites.

Pour into the prepared pans, shaking to spread out the thick batter evenly. Bake until golden and a cake tester comes out clean, 40 to 50 minutes. Let the layers cool in the pans on wire racks for 30 minutes before turning out.

Heat the jam in a small saucepan over low heat until it's runny.

Brush the crumbs off both layers and place one layer on a cake plate. Pour and spread about half the jam over the bottom layer. Top with the second layer and secure it in place with toothpicks. Spread the top with the remaining jam and let it run down the sides of the cake.

Serve with flavored whipped cream if you care to.

Serves 12

OPPOSITE: Set the finished cake aside in a glass cake saver, to show it off while keeping it moist.

FROM FAR LEFT: Use a rubber spatula to fold the beaten whites gently into the batter. You can also use a spatula to spread the jam over the finished cake.

Macaroni Casserole with Chicken and Spicy Sausage

It's probably a toss-up as to which of the two casseroles here is my guests' favorite. You'll just have to try them both and decide for yourself.

NOTE: You'll need to start this casserole a day ahead, because it needs to be refrigerated overnight before baking.

2 tablespoons margarine
¾ pound skinless, boneless chicken breast, cut into small chunks
½ pound andouille sausage or other cured spicy sausage, removed from the
    casings and coarsely chopped
2 cups Tomato Sauce (pages 26–27)
½ pound elbow macaroni
1 cup low-fat cottage cheese
1 pound low-fat cream cheese, at room temperature
¼ cup low-fat sour cream
½ cup minced onion
¾ cup minced red bell pepper
1 tablespoon unsalted butter

Place 1 tablespoon of the margarine in a large skillet over medium-high heat. When it starts to bubble, add the chicken. Sauté, tossing from time to time, until the chicken is done, about 5 minutes. Stir in the sausage and Tomato Sauce. Set aside.

Cook the macaroni according to the package directions and drain. Place the cottage cheese, cream cheese, and sour cream in a bowl and beat with an electric mixer until smooth. Combine with the macaroni and blend well. Stir in the onion and bell pepper. Melt the remaining 1 tablespoon margarine with the butter.

Grease a low-sided 2-quart rectangular baking dish. Cover the bottom of the dish with the macaroni mixture. Drizzle with the melted butter and margarine. Top with the meat-tomato mixture. Cover and refrigerate overnight.

To cook, preheat the oven to 350 degrees. Remove the casserole from the refrigerator while the oven preheats. Bake for 40 minutes, until bubbly.

Serves 8

BELOW: Cut the andouille into 4-inch pieces, quarter the pieces lengthwise, then cut into small chunks.
RIGHT: Again, serve the salad on the same plate as the casserole.

Setting the Table

Casseroles are ideal for outdoor dining. In this case, the table was set in the midst of an ivy-planted terrace.

To set the table we used underliners of old spongeware; dinner plates by Pillivyut; and soup bowls from Bennington Pottery. The flatware is "Vieux-Paris" by Chamblis, and the glasses are Libby's "Gibraltar." All used together with generously sized blue-and-white cotton napkins.

Garden roses and lilacs are mixed in old mustard crocks for a centerpiece. French pressed-glass pitchers were utilized for both the iced tea and beer served with this meal.

CHICKEN D

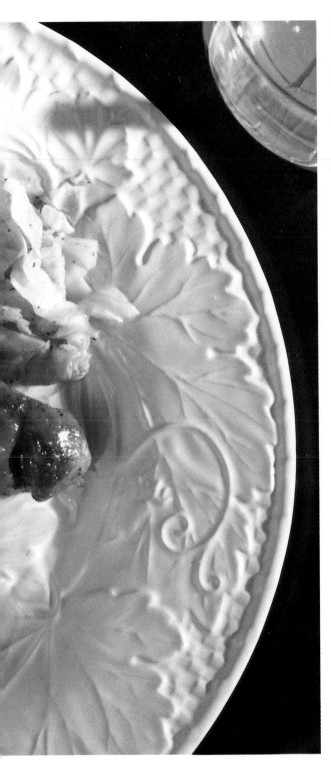

It's really tough to find anyone who dislikes chicken, so obviously chicken is one of your safest bets to build a meal around.

We are going to use chicken breasts in the first menu here because they are quick to cook and require no slicing or fussing. They also happen to be low in calories, so they are even dieter-friendly, if that's a concern.

For the first menu the breasts are sautéed and topped with lemony sour cream sauce, also low-fat. (The sour cream used is the non-butterfat variety.) Accompaniments are creamy baked grits and an absolutely marvelous quick-cooked cabbage. Incidentally, cabbage is used in two other menus in the book. I think it's an underutilized vegetable—and it's very healthful.

Following that course is a simple salad, which could be eliminated if you think the main part of the meal will be enough. And finally, the dessert is a mixed nut tart that's simply delicious, but as I've said, there are plenty of really good ready-made desserts. It's up to you.

The second menu includes that old standby, chicken potpie with a biscuit topping. Its accompaniments are the two found in the pork chapter: chopped winter salad and fresh pineapple chutney. The dessert could be the mixed nut tart, but there is a lemon pudding cake on page 53 that would also be fine with this combination.

The menus were written to serve six, but they're easily expandable.

INNERS

Lemon Chicken with Sour Cream Sauce

The lemon rind and dry roux in this recipe give it its special rich flavor. In total it takes about 45 minutes to complete once you understand the process.

This recipe serves 6 but can easily be increased to serve 8 by adding another chicken breast, cut in half. There'll be plenty of sauce.

Salt and black pepper to taste
4 whole boneless and skinless chicken breasts, each cut in 2 (about 2¾ pounds)
All-purpose flour
2 tablespoons olive oil
1 tablespoon unsalted butter
1½ cups diced onions
1½ cups diced green bell pepper
2 garlic cloves, thinly sliced
Scant ½ teaspoon dried rosemary leaves
2 tablespoons dry roux (see Note)
3 cups chicken stock
2 tablespoons minced lemon zest
¼ cup sour cream substitute

Salt and generously pepper the breast halves and dredge in the flour. Shake off any excess and set aside.

Heat the oil and butter in a large heavy skillet with a lid. Brown the chicken over high heat, about 5 minutes per side. Remove and set aside. Add the onions and bell pepper to the skillet. Turn the heat to medium and cook until the onions are golden, about 8 minutes.

Add the garlic, rosemary, and dry roux; stir to mix. Stir in the stock. Return the chicken and any juice to the skillet. Cover and simmer for 20 minutes, turning once.

Remove the breasts to a warm platter. Add the lemon zest to the sauce, increase the heat to high, and cook for 10 minutes to reduce the sauce. Return the cooked breasts to the pan and simmer for another minute or two, just long enough to heat them through. (If you are pausing here and completing the dish later, add the breasts, cover, and set aside off the heat.) Remove from the heat and stir in the sour cream substitute. Serve with some of the sauce spooned over each portion.

To reheat, simmer just until the breasts are heated through, several minutes, before stirring in the sour cream substitute.

Serves 6

NOTE: Dry roux is very handy, easy to prepare, and keeps for months. Place a cast-iron skillet over high heat until hot. Sprinkle in about ½ cup all-purpose flour, and working quickly, stir the flour around with the edge of a pancake turner (see photograph at right). If the flour is browning too quickly, remove the skillet from the heat momentarily and continue to stir. Cook until the flour is dark gold, about 4 minutes. Do not allow to burn. Remove the dry roux to a bowl as soon as the desired degree of doneness is reached; the flour will continue to cook if left in the hot skillet. When cool, store in a tightly sealed jar. No refrigeration is needed.

PRECEDING PAGES: Lemon Chicken with Sour Cream Sauce, Baked Creamy Grits, and Steamed Green Cabbage.

TOP: Simmer the chicken in the sauce for a few moments, both to heat the chicken and to let it pick up the flavors of the sauce.

ABOVE: The lemon rind should be finely minced with a sharp knife. Make sure you use only the rind; the white pith is bitter.

LEFT: Stir the dry roux with the edge of a pancake turner while you brown it.

Baked Creamy Grits

When you take this out of the oven, drape a dish towel over it. It can sit for 10 to 15 minutes this way.

4½ cups low-fat milk
4 packets chicken stock powder (or 4 chicken bouillon cubes)
1 cup quick (not instant) grits
4 tablespoons (½ stick) unsalted butter
1 teaspoon salt
2 eggs (or an equivalent amount of egg substitute)

Preheat the oven to 400 degrees.

Generously butter a 1½- to 2-quart soufflé dish. Bring 4 cups of the milk slowly to a boil, being careful not to scorch it. Dissolve the chicken stock powder in the milk. Slowly pour in the grits in a steady stream, stirring constantly. Cook over medium heat for 4 minutes, stirring, until thick.

Remove from the heat and add the butter, salt, and the remaining ½ cup milk. Mix well. Add the eggs and mix well. Pour into the prepared soufflé dish.

Bake until lightly brown and puffy, about 45 minutes.

Serves 6 to 8

Steamed Green Cabbage

Many people think they don't particularly like cabbage, maybe because it is so often overcooked. Not so here. These instructions are for the microwave, but you can cook the cabbage, covered, on top of the stove over medium heat.

½ head of green cabbage, cored and coarsely shredded (about 8 cups)
1½ tablespoons rice wine vinegar
½ teaspoon salt
¼ teaspoon black pepper
¼ teaspoon sugar (optional)
2 tablespoons unsalted butter

Place the cabbage in a glass bowl and toss with the vinegar, salt, pepper, and sugar. Cover tightly with plastic wrap. Make a steam hole in the top and microwave on HIGH until crisp-tender, 6 to 8 minutes. Allow to rest, still covered, for several minutes. Toss with the butter.

Serves 6

Mixed Green Salad

While I don't think you necessarily have to serve warm bread with the dinner, I do like some sort of dry melba toast or water biscuits with salad, especially when it is served with cheese. However, again, this is up to you. We served a Saint-André.

VINAIGRETTE
1 tablespoon sherry vinegar
1 tablespoon rice wine vinegar
1 tablespoon fresh lemon juice
¼ cup olive oil
2 tablespoons canola oil
¼ teaspoon salt
¼ teaspoon black pepper
¼ teaspoon dry mustard

9 cups mixed salad greens, washed and dried

Make the vinaigrette. Whisk together all the ingredients and correct the seasoning. Set aside.

Toss the greens with enough vinaigrette to coat the leaves—this may be a bit more than you need. Put on individual serving plates.

Serves 6

OPPOSITE: The Baked Creamy Grits will be nicely browned when done. BELOW, FROM LEFT: Season the cabbage and cover the bowl with plastic wrap. The cooked cabbage should be tender, but still crisp. Whisk the vinaigrette for the salad in a pitcher or measuring cup until emulsified.

Setting the Table

Chicken is an ideal choice for a simple dinner at home because it is the one dish that seems to please everyone.

For this dinner the table is set with tortoiseshell pattern underplates. We then used Portuguese "Vigne" plates for both the salad and main course. In addition to a dinner fork and knife, we set each place with a salad fork and cheese knife. White wine is served in Sasaki's "Classico" wine glasses.

The setting is completed with pink cotton napkins and beeswax candles in an iron candelabra.

For the centerpieces, we cut the stems of pink and white garden roses all the same length and arranged them in a clear glass cylinder. If possible, cut the roses a day ahead to give them time to open up fully.

TOP: Spread the nut filling evenly into the prebaked shell. ABOVE: The tart is rich, so keep the slices small, but don't pass up the flavored whipped cream on top.

Mixed Nut Tart

You might try this with any combination of nuts. The tart is fairly rich, so serve smallish slices.

PASTRY

    1½ cups all-purpose flour
    12 tablespoons (1½ sticks) chilled unsalted butter, cut into 8 pieces
    Pinch of salt
    1 tablespoon sugar
    3 to 4 tablespoons ice water

FILLING

    1½ cups sugar
    ⅓ cup water
    ⅛ teaspoon cream of tartar
    1¼ cups heavy cream, heated
    ¼ cup honey
    1 cup *each* pecans, walnuts, and blanched almonds, coarsely chopped
    1½ tablespoons grated orange zest

TOPPING

    1 cup heavy cream, chilled
    1 tablespoon sugar
    1 tablespoon brandy (or orange-flavored liqueur)
    1½ teaspoons grated orange zest

Make the pastry. Place the flour, butter, salt, and sugar in a food processor and pulse several times to cut in the butter. Sprinkle the water over all and continue pulsing the machine until just before a ball begins to form. Turn the pastry out and gather it into a ball. Flatten the ball between 2 sheets of waxed paper. Refrigerate for about 45 minutes.

Meanwhile, preheat the oven to 375 degrees.

Place the chilled dough on a floured board and roll out into a large round. Fit into a 9-inch tart pan or pie pan. Fold the edges under and crimp decoratively. Prick the bottom with the tines of a fork. Line the pastry shell with foil and weigh down with pie weights or dried beans. Bake for 20 minutes, until set. Carefully remove the foil and weights and set aside.

Make the filling. Combine the sugar, water, and cream of tartar in a heavy pot and cook over medium-high heat, stirring until the sugar melts. Boil, without stirring, until the mixture caramelizes to a light caramel color, about 9 minutes. Remove the pot from the heat and carefully stir in the heated cream. Return to the heat and cook, stirring, until well blended, 2 minutes. Remove from the heat and stir in the honey, nuts, and orange zest.

Pour the filling into the pastry shell. Bake until the crust is browned and the filling is bubbly (the center will be on the jiggly side), about 30 minutes. Cool on a rack.

Make the topping. In a chilled bowl, whip the cream with the sugar until soft peaks form. Beat in the brandy and orange zest.

Serves 10 to 12

Time Plan

Start with the dessert. While the pastry is resting, wash and dry the salad greens. Roll them in a clean towel and keep them in the refrigerator. Make the vinaigrette.

Cut the cabbage and place it in as large a bowl as will fit in your microwave. Leave this out until you are ready to cook it. Toss with the other ingredients just before cooking.

Next make the dry roux.

Now get back to the pie. Roll the pastry and while it's baking, make the filling. While the pie is baking, whip the cream, put it in a metal strainer over a bowl, and keep it in the refrigerator.

Next brown the chicken and cook the vegetables; add the seasonings and roux as well as the chicken stock. Return the chicken to the pan and cook for 20 minutes. Remember to turn the breasts while they are cooking.

Preheat the oven for the grits. Slowly bring the milk to a boil and grease a soufflé dish. Cook the grits on top of the stove and then put it in to bake.

About 10 to 15 minutes before the grits is done, finish assembling the cabbage and put it in the microwave to cook. It will have time to rest as you finish the chicken. Add the lemon zest and begin to reduce the sauce for the chicken. Add the chicken to reheat and finish with the sour cream substitute.

All that will be left to do is the tossing and plating of the salad just before you serve it.

Chicken Pot Pie with Biscuit Topping

When I make chicken pot pie, I usually cook the chicken a day ahead.

12 celery ribs
1 6-pound hen
Generous 1½ cups sliced carrot
Generous 1½ cups diced (½-inch) potato
3 tablespoons margarine
3 tablespoons unsalted butter
¾ cup dry roux (page 36)
2 tablespoons all-purpose flour
1 teaspoon salt, plus extra for salting layers
Generous ½ teaspoon pepper
1 very large onion, coarsely chopped and dry caramelized (see Note)
14 dashes Tabasco sauce
1½ cups frozen baby lima beans

BISCUIT TOPPING
2½ cups all-purpose flour
1¼ teaspoons salt
2½ teaspoons baking powder
½ teaspoon baking soda
4 tablespoons (½ stick) unsalted butter
4 tablespoons (½ stick) margarine
1½ cups buttermilk

Break the celery into pieces and stuff the hen with some of them. Place the hen in a deep pot just large enough to hold it and cover it with water. Add the remaining celery. Cover and simmer for 1½ hours, or until tender.

Allow to cool in the stock and then refrigerate until well chilled. Degrease the stock. Remove the meat from the bones and set aside. Return the bones to the stock in the pot and cook at a gentle boil until reduced to 6 cups, about 45 minutes to 1 hour. Set aside.

Put the carrot slices in a small saucepan and cover with water. Bring to a simmer and cook for 4 minutes. Drain and set aside. Put the diced potato in a small saucepan, cover with salted water, bring to a boil, and cook for 7 minutes. Drain and set aside.

Preheat the oven to 450 degrees. Grease a 12 × 9 × 2-inch baking dish and set aside. Strain the stock and reheat.

Combine the margarine and butter in a large skillet over medium heat. Sprinkle in the roux and stir to mix well. Whisk in 5 cups of the hot stock. Put the flour in a small bowl. Add about 1 cup of the heated stock and whisk to make sure there are no lumps. Add this to the sauce and simmer, whisking, until thickened, about 5 minutes. When smooth add the salt, pepper, and Tabasco. Simmer for 1 minute.

Put a layer of chicken in the bottom of the baking dish and top with one-third of the carrots, potatoes, and onions. Sprinkle with salt (and a litle pepper if you like). Continue layering until all the chicken and vegetables are used, finishing with the chicken. Top with the lima beans. Pour the sauce over all.

Make the biscuits. Mix the flour, salt, baking powder, and baking soda in a large bowl. Cut in the butter and margarine with 2 knives or a pastry blender to

FAR LEFT: Leave a little space between the biscuits to give them room to rise and brown. LEFT: Use a metal spatula to turn the onions as they brown. BELOW: Plan for each guest to get at least two biscuits.

about the size of large peas. Quickly stir in the buttermilk. Gather the dough into a ball and turn out onto a floured surface. Pat or roll out about ⅜ inch thick. Cut into about twenty 2½-inch biscuits with a floured cutter. Place the biscuits on the assembled pie, leaving space between each—4 across and 5 down.

Bake until the biscuits are golden and cooked, about 30 minutes. Put a foil-lined pan on the shelf below the baking dish as it sometimes bubbles over.

Serves 8 to 10

NOTE: To make the caramelized onions, place a large cast-iron skillet over high heat until very hot. Add the onions and cook, without stirring, 4 to 5 minutes until they get brown. Use a metal spatula to turn them and brown the other side, about 4 minutes more. (See photograph above).

These may be done several days in advance and stored, tightly covered, in the refrigerator.

It is important to chop the onions by hand. If you do them in a food processor they will give off too much liquid.

FISH DINN

When it comes to cooking fish, as far as I'm concerned, the less you do the better it is. So my formula is pretty simple: I like fish filleted, sprinkled with a few aromatic herbs, dotted with butter, and then quickly baked or broiled and finished off with a squeeze of fresh lemon. It seems every recipe I truly like is some variation of this basic method.

Both of these menus start with a light combination of Boursin and ricotta cheeses that is baked and served with a garnish of fresh tomatoes and shiny black olives—very tasty and easy to prepare. Then comes the main course—one of my favorite baked fish variations—accompanied by a mixed grain pilaf and a simple and tasty fresh relish. I think you'll find many uses for the pilaf because not only is it a perfect accompaniment to a vast variety of other dishes, but it practically invites innovation. Ditto the fresh relish. So, let your imagination loose.

As for the dessert, it is definitely among my all-time favorites—an old-fashioned lemon pudding cake embellished with fresh berries. Any kind of berries will do, but this time I opted for raspberries.

For the second menu, I've marinated the fish in a kind of teriyaki sauce, and then grilled it. For accompaniments, there's plain old buttered rice with parsley and the vegetable salad from the seafood chapter. And the lemon pudding cake goes along just fine.

All told, two very nice meals for six.

ERS

PRECEDING PAGES: Serve the Grilled Teriyaki Snapper (recipe, page 54) over buttered rice. ABOVE: Garnish the Tomatoes with Baked Cheeses with oil-cured olives. BELOW: Beat the Boursin and ricotta until very smooth.

Tomatoes with Baked Cheeses

Should the tomatoes in the market not look too appetizing, use cherry tomatoes, cut in half. They usually have a better flavor than the larger but underripened ones.

1 5-ounce package Boursin cheese with pepper
Part-skim ricotta cheese
2 egg whites
5 tablespoons olive oil
1 tablespoon balsamic vinegar
½ teaspoon salt or to taste
Black pepper to taste
3 medium tomatoes, halved and thickly sliced
30 oil-cured black olives

Preheat the oven to 350 degrees. Butter an 8½ × 4½-inch loaf pan.

Place the Boursin in a large measuring cup and add enough ricotta to make 2 cups. Place the cheeses in a medium bowl and beat in the egg whites. Scrape the mixture into the loaf pan and smooth the top. Drizzle with 2 tablespoons of the olive oil. Bake for 40 minutes, until the mixture puffs slightly and is firm to the touch. Remove from the oven and cool on a rack.

When room temperature, loosen around the edges with a knife and turn the baked cheeses out onto a deep dish. Pour any pan juices over the top.

Meanwhile, make a vinaigrette by whisking the remaining 3 tablespoons of olive oil with the vinegar, salt, and pepper.

To serve, place several slices of tomato on each of 6 individual salad plates. Sprinkle each serving with 5 olives and drizzle with a bit of the vinaigrette. Cut the baked cheeses into 6 portions and place on the tomatoes. Top the whole thing with a grind or two of black pepper.

Serves 6

Baked Fish Fillets

When you test fish for doneness, be sure you test the thickest part of the largest fillet you are cooking. A minute or two can make the difference between a properly cooked fish and an underdone one.

6 mild white fish fillets, such as lemon sole (each about 6 ounces)
6 tablespoons soy sauce
1 tablespoon canola oil
Black pepper to taste
¼ cup finely chopped green onion
¼ cup coarsely chopped fresh dill (no stems)
3 tablespoons chilled unsalted butter, cut into 18 or more small pieces
Fresh lemon juice
Lemon wedges

Preheat the oven to 350 degrees. Line 2 low-sided baking pans with foil and spray with vegetable oil spray.

Place the fillets, skin side down, on a sheet of waxed paper and rub each generously with soy sauce, using about 1 tablespoon of soy on each. Rub lightly with the oil. Place the fillets, skin side down, in the prepared baking pans and season with pepper to taste. Toss the green onion and dill together and sprinkle each fillet with an equal amount. Dot with the butter, then squeeze a little lemon juice over each.

Bake for about 15 minutes, or until the fish just starts to flake. Serve on heated plates with a wedge or two of lemon. (See photograph on page 50.)

Serves 6

LEFT: The pan is lined with oiled foil so the fillets won't stick. Dot each piece of fish with butter before baking.

Pasta and Grain Pilaf

The bulgur wheat gives this pilaf a distinctive nutty flavor I know you'll like. Leftovers can be reheated, wrapped, in the microwave oven or wrapped in foil and heated in a very slow oven.

3 tablespoons unsalted butter
½ cup minced onion
¼ cup minced red bell pepper
¼ cup minced celery
1 tablespoon minced shallots
½ cup long-grain white rice
½ cup bulgur wheat
½ cup dried spaghetti, broken into small pieces
3 cups chicken stock, heated
½ teaspoon salt
¼ teaspoon black pepper

Preheat the oven to 350 degrees.

Melt the butter in a skillet over medium heat; add the onion and cook until wilted, about 3 minutes. Add the bell pepper, celery, and shallots and sauté for 2 minutes, to coat well with oil. Add the rice, bulgur, and spaghetti pieces; cook, stirring, for 2 minutes. Add the stock, salt, and pepper and bring to a boil. Pour into a 1½- to 2-quart casserole with a tight lid. Bake, covered, until all the liquid is absorbed, about 30 minutes.

Serves 6

The first thing to do is to make the Lemon Pudding Cake. I make it the day before and chill it overnight.

Next up is the baked cheeses for the first course. Once you have this baked, leave it at room temperature until you are ready to serve it—it doesn't taste as good if you refrigerate it.

Now get started on the relish. The cucumbers take 1 hour to drain with the salt. Cut all the other vegetables while they drain. Then all you'll have to do is toss toss, mix mix. Another option is to make the relish the day before and refrigerate it.

Next prepare the fish for baking. You can hold the fish for up to an hour, covered with plastic wrap, at room temperature. If you are keeping it longer than that, put it in the refrigerator and plan on adding another few minutes of baking time.

Now's the time to get the Pasta and Grain Pilaf under way. You have two options here. The first is to sauté the vegetables in advance. Then, before you sit down to the first course, add the rice, bulgur, and spaghetti, then the stock, and put it in the oven to bake for half an hour. The second option is to make it all in advance and hold it, covered—or reheat it with the fish.

Just before you call everyone to the table for the first course, put the fish in to bake.

OPPOSITE: Put some of the Pasta and Grain Pilaf on each side of the Baked Fish Fillets. Lemon wedges are a good garnish. ABOVE: Once the pasta and grains have cooked in the oil, stir in the stock.

Fresh Relish

This relish adds a snap of flavor to whatever it is served with. Keep it in mind for picnic fare, like baked ham or cold chicken.

1 cup diced, peeled, and seeded cucumber
1 teaspoon coarse salt
¾ cup diced celery
1¾ cups diced radishes
1 to 2 tablespoons minced jalapeño chili pepper (no seeds)
2 tablespoons minced parsley
2 tablespoons olive oil
2 tablespoons white wine vinegar
Pepper to taste

Place the cucumber in a bowl and toss with the salt. Transfer to a colander and allow to drain in the sink for 1 hour.

Place the cucumber in a bowl and toss with the celery, radishes, jalapeño pepper, and parsley. Whisk together the olive oil and vinegar and toss with the vegetables. Refrigerate until ready to use. Add a little more salt and pepper if necessary.

Serves 6

You can use your hands to toss the ingredients for the Fresh Relish.

Lemon Pudding Cake

You can serve this dessert either warm or chilled, and I can't really say which I like best. There is, however, an advantage to serving the cake chilled: you can make it a day in advance. The trick here is to allow the cake to cool completely on a rack before you refrigerate it.

4 tablespoons (½ stick) unsalted butter, softened

1½ cups sugar

4 eggs, separated

3 tablespoons all-purpose flour

1¾ cups milk

½ cup fresh lemon juice

1½ tablespoons grated lemon zest

Preheat the oven to 350 degrees. Generously butter a 2-quart soufflé dish.

Cream together the butter and sugar until light and fluffy. Add the egg yolks, one at a time, beating well after each addition. Stir in the flour, combining well. Pour in one-third of the milk and stir until smooth, then stir in the remaining milk. Stir in the lemon juice and zest.

In a very clean, deep bowl, beat the egg whites until stiff peaks form. Fold the beaten whites into the batter. Pour into the prepared soufflé dish. Place the soufflé dish in a larger baking pan and pour boiling water into the large pan to reach about 1 inch up the side of the soufflé dish. Bake until golden and puffy, about 1 hour. Cool on a rack.

If you are going to chill the cake, keep it on the rack, covered with a tea towel, for at least 1 hour, or until at room temperature. Cover tightly with plastic wrap and refrigerate for several hours or overnight. Serve from the dish.

Serves 6

ABOVE: Spoon a bit of the puddinglike center over the cakey top when you serve this dessert. Garnish with raspberries.
BELOW: Pour the batter into a buttered soufflé dish.

Grilled Teriyaki Snapper

You can substitute any firm fish fillet in this dish if snapper isn't available.

⅓ cup soy sauce
1 thick slice of fresh ginger, peeled and chopped
2 tablespoons dry sherry
1 tablespoon sugar
2 garlic cloves, minced
1 2½-pound piece of snapper fillet, 1 inch at its thickest, cut into 6 pieces
3 tablespoons unsalted butter, cut into 6 pieces

Preheat the broiler.

In small bowl, whisk together the soy, ginger, sherry, sugar, and garlic. Place the fish in a single layer in a shallow dish and pour the marinade over the fish. Set aside, covered, for 30 minutes, turning the fish several times.

Broil the fish about 5 minutes per side, until well browned and flaky, basting once on each side with the marinade.

Place the fish on individual plates and top each serving with a bit of butter. (See the photograph on page 46–47.)

Serves 6

ABOVE: Once the fish is in the marinade, cover it and set it aside for 30 minutes.

Setting the Table

Here again is a table setting composed of heirlooms. Some of the pieces have a vaguely Greek theme, as expressed in the antique creamware candlesticks and the 18th-century Danish dinner plates. The gold-rimmed glasses and shell pattern silverware, which complete the setting, are antique as well. Complementing it all is a set of yellow damask linens.

For a centerpiece, a variety of compotes—one in the same pattern as the dinner plate—has been filled with peaches, nectarines, and grapes. Nestled between them is a large bunch of mint placed in a celadon urn—for both color and fragrance.

PASTA DIN

While looking through some notes I had made on Italian food a brief ten years ago, I was astonished to be reminded just how much our understanding and attitudes have changed toward this immensely popular cuisine. Time was when Italian cooking, in most folks' minds, meant some version of spaghetti and meatballs. This, of course, was long before spaghetti was rechristened "pasta."

However, slowly but surely, it began to dawn on us that pasta could be topped with anything from a simple tomato sauce to a well-seasoned lamb "stew" with cabbage—something that might never occur to the average Italian.

The menu begins with grilled portobello mushrooms accompanied by black olives and tomatoes. This combination is so tasty that I have been known to make an entire meal of it alone! The pasta has a meltingly good onion sauce tossed with spring vegetables. (You can adapt this onion sauce to make other vegetable sauces.) Generous helpings of garlic bread are the natural go-along. Then it's finished off with a dessert that's a favorite of all my guests—fresh peaches and cream cake.

The second menu features my spicy lamb and cabbage pasta, guaranteed to please the most discriminating. And then I'm including a recipe for the best and simplest pasta sauce going. It calls for canned jalapeño chili peppers (fresh won't do) and you can have it ready by the time the pasta is cooked.

These meals will serve six—four if you're hungry.

NERS

Grilled Portobello Mushrooms with Black Olives and Tomatoes

If you don't have an outdoor grill handy, do the mushrooms under the broiler. You might also want to try this with sliced domestic white or brown mushrooms sautéed in a little hot oil (see the Pasta with Lamb Sauce and Cabbage, page 66). However, the texture of portobellos is especially well suited to this dish.

18 small whole shallots, peeled
¼ cup plus 3 tablespoons olive oil
1 head of garlic
Salt and black pepper to taste
3 large portobello mushrooms (about 12 ounces total weight)
2 tablespoons drained capers
24 oil-cured black olives
2 tablespoons red wine vinegar
2 large tomatoes, cut into wedges

Preheat the oven to 350 degrees.

Rub the shallots with 1 tablespoon of the oil. Wrap them all in foil in a single package. Slice the top off the head of garlic to expose the cloves, rub with 1 tablespoon of the oil, and lightly sprinkle with salt and pepper. Wrap in foil. Place the shallots and garlic in the oven and roast for an hour or more, until tender. Set aside.

Meanwhile, prepare an outdoor grill or preheat the broiler.

Remove the stems from the mushrooms and discard. Brush the mushrooms with 1 tablespoon of the oil and grill until tender, 4 to 5 minutes per side. Remove to a cutting board and cut into medium dice.

Place the mushrooms in a bowl and toss with the capers, olives, and roasted shallots. Squeeze the roasted garlic out of the skins and into the bowl with the mushroom mixture. In a small bowl, whisk the remaining ¼ cup oil and the vinegar together. Pour over the other ingredients in the bowl and toss.

Mound in the center of a serving plate and surround with the tomato wedges.

Serves 6

PRECEDING PAGES: **The Pasta with Onion Sauce and Spring Vegetables is sprinkled with a mixture of goat cheese and bread crumbs.**

TOP: The Grilled Portobello Mushrooms are served surrounded by a ring of tomato wedges. ABOVE: The mushrooms will taste best grilled outdoors, but you can also do this under the broiler.

Pasta with Onion Sauce and Spring Vegetables

Other fresh vegetable combinations can be used instead of the asparagus, such as green onions and squash—both blanched as you would the asparagus.

4 tablespoons (½ stick) unsalted butter
⅓ cup plus 1 tablespoon olive oil
5 cups coarsely chopped onions
Generous ⅓ cup fine fresh bread crumbs, toasted (see Note)
3 ounces creamy mild chèvre
Salt
1 pound dried fettuccine
¾ pound asparagus, trimmed
1 large yellow bell pepper, seeded and cut into thin slices

Heat the butter and ⅓ cup of the olive oil in a heavy skillet over medium heat. Add the onions and cook, stirring occasionally, until golden and slightly browned, 10 to 15 minutes. Set aside.

In a small bowl, combine the bread crumbs and the chèvre with a fork until crumbly (see the photograph below center). Set aside.

Bring a large pot of water to a boil. Salt the water and cook the fettuccine according to package directions.

Meanwhile, bring a medium pot of water to a boil. Salt the water and blanch the asparagus for 3 minutes. Drain and plunge into cold water. Pat dry and cut diagonally into ½-inch pieces. Set aside. (This can be done before you put on the fettuccine if you think the timing is too tight.)

Heat the remaining 1 tablespoon olive oil in a medium skillet over medium heat. Toss in the yellow bell pepper and cook, stirring, until the pepper starts to get tender, about 3 minutes. Add the asparagus and cook, tossing, for another minute or so, until heated through.

Drain the pasta and return it to the cooking pot. Toss with the onions and divide among 6 warm plates. Top each serving with the asparagus and bell peppers, using it all. Sprinkle with the chèvre–bread crumb mixture. (See the photograph on pages 56–57.)

Serves 6

NOTE: Fresh bread crumbs are best for this dish. To make them, remove the crusts from a slice of good white bread and run the bread through a food processor to make fine crumbs. Toast them in a dry skillet over medium heat, stirring, until they're golden brown, 5 to 7 minutes.

BELOW, FROM LEFT: As the onions for the sauce start to cook, they will become glossy and soft. Crumble the chèvre into the bread crumbs for the topping. Use two large forks to toss the fettuccine with the onion sauce in the cooking pot. OPPOSITE: Add the asparagus to the yellow pepper and heat through. OVERLEAF: The Garlic Bread, ready for baking.

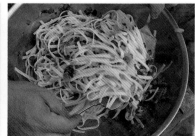

Garlic Bread

This is how they make garlic bread at the famous Commander's Palace restaurant in New Orleans. It has been a favorite there for years.

1 loaf French bread (about 14 inches long)
8 tablespoons (1 stick) unsalted butter (or a combination of butter and
    margarine)
2 garlic cloves, mashed to a puree
¼ cup finely chopped fresh dill
¼ cup freshly grated Parmesan cheese

Preheat the oven to 375 degrees.

Slice the bread lengthwise. Melt the butter in a small skillet, add the garlic, and heat gently for 2 minutes. Do not brown. Brush the garlic-butter mixture generously over the cut sides of the bread halves. Sprinkle with the dill and cheese. Place on a baking sheet and bake until golden, 5 to 8 minutes. Cut each half crosswise into 1-inch slices.

Serves 6

Time Plan

Begin with the Peaches and Cream Cake. When the cake has been assembled, refrigerate it until dessert time. (Obviously, you could do this several hours in advance.)

Next, turn your attention to the mushrooms. Put the shallots and garlic in the oven, and proceed with the rest of the recipe. It's okay to let this sit at room temperature for an hour or so.

Next, assemble the Garlic Bread and keep it covered with plastic wrap until it's time to bake it. You'll want to serve it hot.

You can't really finish the pasta until you're ready to eat it, but you can have things ready. Start with the onions. While they are browning, toast the bread crumbs and mix them with the chèvre. Blanch and cool the asparagus and cut the yellow pepper.

Often, when I'm having a dinner party, I precook the pasta. Here's how. Once it's *almost* al dente, drain the pasta and run it under cold water to completely stop the cooking process. Drain it and toss it with a little bit of olive oil. Then, when you sit down to your first course, put a pot of water on to boil. Reheat the cooked pasta in the boiling water. (It takes under a minute to reheat, so be careful not to overcook it.) And then complete the sauce and bake the garlic bread.

Peaches and Cream Cake

The cake is very fine and densely textured—a perfect foil for peaches and cream.

PEACH FILLING

    5 or 6 large ripe peaches

    Juice of ½ lemon

    2 tablespoons sugar

CAKE

    2 cups sifted all-purpose flour

    ⅓ cup cornstarch or potato starch

    2 teaspoons baking powder

    ¾ teaspoon salt

    12 tablespoons (1½ sticks) unsalted butter, softened

    1⅓ cups sugar

    ¾ cup milk

    1½ teaspoons vanilla extract

    9 large egg whites

CREAM FILLING

    2 cups heavy cream

    ½ cup sugar

    1½ teaspoons vanilla extract

Make the peach filling. Dip the peaches in boiling water for 30 seconds, then place in a bowl of ice water. Slip off the skins; cut each peach into about 12 slices. Discard the skins and stones. Place the peach slices in a large bowl, toss with the lemon juice and sugar, and set aside.

Make the cake. Preheat the oven to 350 degrees. Generously grease two 9-inch round cake pans; line the bottoms with waxed paper. Grease the paper and flour it lightly, shaking out any excess. Set aside.

Sift the flour with the cornstarch, baking powder, and salt. Set aside.

Cream the butter with the sugar until fluffy. Add the dry mixture in 4 parts, alternating with the milk and ending with the flour. Stir in the vanilla.

In a deep, clean bowl, beat the egg whites until soft peaks form. Gently fold the beaten whites into the batter. Pour the batter into the prepared pans. Bake in the center of the oven for 20 to 25 minutes, until a cake tester comes out clean. Cool the cakes in the pans on racks for about 10 minutes. Turn out the cakes onto racks and let cool completely, about 1 hour.

Make the cream filling. Combine the cream, sugar, and vanilla in a large chilled bowl. Whip with an electric mixer until soft peaks form.

Assemble the cake. Place 1 cake layer, bottom side up, on a serving platter or cake dish. The peaches will have given up a bit of juice by now, so spoon some of it over the bottom layer, a little at a time to allow it to soak in. Put half of the peach slices on this layer and cover with about half of the whipped cream. Top with the other cake layer, top side up. Spoon the remaining cream over this layer and spoon on the remaining peaches. You can hold the layers together with toothpicks if you need to.

Keep the cake refrigerated, very loosely covered with foil or plastic wrap, until ready to serve.

Serves 12

TOP: The Peaches and Cream Cake is served on a clear glass cake stand. ABOVE LEFT: Place the first layer bottom side up on the cake stand. The juice from the peaches should soak into the bottom layer of the cake; top with a big spoonful of cream filling. ABOVE RIGHT: You don't need to spread the filling over the peaches before placing the top layer. Place this layer top side up.

Pasta with Lamb Sauce and Cabbage

This is an all-in-one dinner, and a very hearty one at that. You don't really need anything but bread and wine with it, but why not add a salad and dessert? My choice for a chilly night.

LAMB SAUCE

1 ounce dried porcini mushrooms

2 cups hot tap water

½ cup plus 2 tablespoons olive oil

8 cups sliced onions

3½ tablespoons minced garlic (about 10 cloves)

½ pound white mushrooms, sliced

1½ pounds very well trimmed lamb shoulder or leg (about 2¼ pounds boned but untrimmed)

Salt and black pepper to taste

Flour, for dredging

1½ cups dry white wine, warmed

2 cups beef stock, warmed

1 large bay leaf

5 4-inch fresh rosemary sprigs

HOT OIL

1 tablespoon crushed red pepper flakes

½ cup olive oil

CABBAGE

1 large head of cabbage (about 2 pounds), cored and shredded

3 tablespoons rice wine vinegar

1 teaspoon salt

1 teaspoon black pepper

ASSEMBLY

1 pound dried penne

Make the lamb sauce. Place the porcini in a medium bowl and cover with the water. Allow to sit for at least 1 hour. Drain, reserving the liquid. Remove the tough stems and coarsely chop the mushrooms. Pour the liquid through 2 layers of dampened cheesecloth to remove any grit; set aside.

Heat ¼ cup of the oil in a large skillet over high heat. Add the onions and sauté until browned, about 12 minutes. Add the garlic and sauté for 1 minute. Use a slotted spoon to remove the onions and garlic to a large bowl; set aside.

RIGHT: **Crushed red pepper and olive oil are combined for the hot oil. Strain this before using it.** OPPOSITE: **The pasta has been tossed with hot oil and topped with the cabbage and the lamb sauce.**

Add 2 tablespoons of oil to the pan. Add the mushrooms and sauté until golden, about 2 minutes. Remove and add to the onion mixture; set aside.

Place the lamb in a large bowl and season liberally with salt and pepper. Toss with flour until well coated.

Add the remaining ¼ cup oil to the skillet and set over a high heat until almost smoking. Add the lamb in batches and cook until well browned. As the meat browns, add it to the bowl with the onions and mushrooms.

When all of the meat is browned, return it to the skillet. Add the porcini and their soaking liquid, the onions, garlic, and sautéed mushrooms from the bowl, the wine, beef stock, bay leaf, and rosemary. Bring to a boil. Lower the heat to a simmer, cover, and cook very slowly for 2 hours, stirring occasionally. Remove the lid and simmer for 1 hour more, or until the meat is falling apart and the sauce is thick. If the lamb sauce is too thick, thin it with a little water or stock. Taste for salt and pepper.

Make the hot oil. Combine the crushed red pepper and oil in a small saucepan over medium heat. When the oil is hot and almost smoking, remove it from the heat and set aside to cool. Strain before using, discarding the pepper flakes.

Make the cabbage. Place the cabbage in a glass bowl. Toss in the remaining ingredients. Cover tightly with plastic wrap. Make a steam hole in the top and microwave on HIGH until crisp-tender, about 5 minutes. Allow to rest, still covered, for another several minutes. If not cooked enough to your taste, cook slightly longer, but it should not be too limp. (You can also steam the cabbage until crisp-tender and toss it with the vinegar, salt, and pepper.)

Assemble the dish. Bring a large pot of water to a boil. Salt the water and add the penne. Cook until al dente. Drain well.

Toss the penne with 2 to 4 tablespoons of the strained hot oil (reserve any leftover oil for another use) and the cooked cabbage. Divide among 6 warmed serving plates and top with the lamb sauce. Do not serve with cheese.

Serves 6

Tomato-Jalapeño Sauce

Here's a bonus recipe. The quantity of pickled jalapeños called for here makes a very hot sauce, so reduce it if you don't like your sauce fiery. The sauce also has the advantage of being very quick and easy to prepare. It's best with a sturdy pasta, like penne.

2 medium tomatoes
2 tablespoons olive oil
2 tablespoons minced garlic
2 tablespoons seeded and finely chopped pickled jalapeño chili peppers
Salt and black pepper to taste

Peel the tomatoes. Place a strainer over a small bowl. Halve the tomatoes and squeeze out the seeds into the strainer. Press on the seeds to get out the juice. Discard the seeds. Dice the tomatoes and mix with the juice.

Heat the oil in a skillet over medium heat. Add the garlic and jalapeños and sauté until fragrant, 2 or 3 minutes. Reduce the heat to low. Add the tomatoes and juices and simmer until slightly thickened, about 5 minutes. Season with salt and pepper.

Makes enough sauce for 12 to 16 ounces dried pasta

ABOVE: **Freshly grated Parmesan would be a nice accompaniment to Penne with Tomato-Jalapeño Sauce.** RIGHT: **Sauté the garlic and jalapeños until fragrant.**

Setting the Table

Dinners at home don't always have to be in the dining room, and the backyard doesn't have to be for barbecues only. Here, a nice casual dinner is served under the trees.

The green underplate, dessert plate, and salad bowl (for the grilled mushrooms and tomatoes) are from Terre d'Hautanboul. The white dinner plate is called "Almost Round." The picnic napkin is Irish linen, and the flatware is from the Martha Stewart collection for Kmart. Kaj Franck carafes hold red wine.

For a centerpiece, four Pilsner glasses were filled with a little bit of everything from the garden—from black-eyed Susans to day lilies to roses—and arranged around the umbrella pole.

PORK DIN

As we slowly became aware of cholesterol counts and what those counts meant for our health, our dreams of pork roasts glistening under richly browned fat began to make us feel guilty. So many of us "did the right thing"—and passed on pork.

Well, luckily, there's a happy ending, for along the way, farmers have learned how to give us leaner pork. So now if we trim the fat, we can stop dreaming and enjoy the real thing—without having to feel we should do penance.

The first menu here starts with a cold sweet potato soup based on the classic vichyssoise. I'll bet you find this a very useful addition to your cooking files. This is followed by moist roast loin of pork accompanied by fresh pineapple chutney and a chopped "winter" salad. I think a warm multigrain or sourdough dinner roll (store-bought) would be nice with this. And for dessert I've revived and added to another classic cake—chocolate pudding cake. I'm such a fan of pudding cakes because they're so easy to prepare and serve—and they taste so good!

The second menu utilizes the same cut of pork, but this time it's cut into medallions, sautéed, and finished with port and prunes. There are lots of choices as far as accompaniments, but I've suggested a baked potato dish and grated baked beets. However, the possibilities are pretty flexible. The baked creamy grits and steamed green cabbage from the chicken menu (page 36) would also be nice.

These menus are designed for six.

NERS

Sweet Potato Vichyssoise

Quick, easy, and tasty!

3 cups peeled and sliced sweet potatoes
1¾ cups sliced green onions, mostly white part
5 cups chicken stock (more or less)
Salt and white pepper to taste
½ cup half-and-half
Chives (optional)

Place the sweet potatoes and green onions in a medium saucepan. Add enough chicken stock to cover the potatoes and bring to a boil over high heat. Reduce the heat to low and simmer until tender, about 15 minutes. Allow to cool for several minutes, then strain, reserving the liquid. Puree the solids in a food processor or put through a food mill and return to the saucepan with the reserved liquid. Taste for salt and pepper. Simmer a few minutes, then set aside off the heat until cool. Refrigerate, covered, until chilled.

To serve, stir in the half-and-half. Place in chilled soup bowls. Garnish each serving with some snipped chives if you like.

Serves 6 to 8

Roasted Pork Loin with Pan Juices

Be sure you start out with the meat at room temperature.

1 2½-pound loin of pork, boned and tied
Salt to taste
1 teaspoon black pepper
1 tablespoon olive oil
2 cups chicken stock
2 tablespoons all-purpose flour
1 tablespoon butter, softened

Preheat the oven to 450 degrees.

Sprinkle the loin with the salt and pepper. Heat the oil in a heavy ovenproof skillet over medium-high heat. Brown the meat on all sides. Place in the oven. Roast until an internal temperature of 155 degrees is reached, 30 to 35 minutes, turning once. Remove it to a cutting board and cover it loosely with foil.

While the meat is roasting, heat the chicken stock and mash the flour and butter together in a small bowl.

Place the skillet you cooked the pork in over medium-high heat. Add the stock to deglaze the skillet, stirring to dissolve any browned bits. When the sauce has come to a boil, add bits of the butter-flour mixture, stirring, to thicken the sauce.

To serve, cut the meat into thick slices and top with a spoon or two of the sauce. (See the photographs on pages 70–71 and 74.)

Serves 6

PRECEDING PAGES: Cut the pork loin evenly in fairly thick slices. OPPOSITE: Snip chives as a garnish for the Sweet Potato Vichyssoise. LEFT: The stock should cover the sweet potatoes.

Fresh Pineapple Chutney

As you might imagine, this is marvelous with curry. But it's also a great foil for simply roasted meats.

1 cup tightly packed dark brown sugar

⅔ cup white wine vinegar

⅓ cup fresh lime juice

½ cup coarsely chopped onion

2 large shallots, peeled and thinly sliced

⅓ cup peeled and coarsely chopped fresh ginger

1 cinnamon stick, 2 or 3 inches long

1 tablespoon mustard seeds

1 teaspoon crushed red pepper

2 cups fresh pineapple, cut into ¾-inch chunks

Combine all the ingredients except the pineapple in a nonreactive saucepan. Bring quickly to a boil over high heat, cover, and turn the heat to low. Simmer for 15 minutes. Uncover the pan and turn the heat up. Boil gently to thicken and reduce the liquid slightly, 5 to 10 minutes.

Remove the pan from the heat and stir in the pineapple. Return to the heat and simmer for another 4 minutes, until thick. Cool to room temperature, then refrigerate, covered, until chilled.

Makes about 2 cups

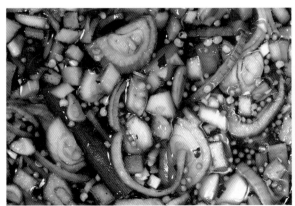

OPPOSITE: The main course—Roasted Pork Loin, Fresh Pineapple Chutney, and Chopped Winter Salad. FAR LEFT: The chutney ingredients, before they have reduced. LEFT: Stir in the pineapple off the heat.

Time Plan

Begin with the cake. Once it's in the oven you can get going on the soup and chutney.

While the cake's baking, put the potatoes and onions for the soup on to cook. When they're tender, set them aside to cool and turn your attention to the chutney. After the chutney is cooked and cooling, puree the soup, season it, and finish the cooking. Allow the soup and chutney to cool to room temperature, then refrigerate.

Next, chop and combine all the salad ingredients and place them, covered, in the refrigerator. Mix the dressing and refrigerate it, covered.

Make the Chocolate Whipped Cream and refrigerate that too.

Take the pork out of the refrigerator and preheat the oven before your guests arrive. As you plan your timing, remember that the meat will take 5 or 6 minutes to sear, 30 minutes or so to cook, and another 5 minutes of resting time before you carve it.

Combine the softened butter and flour at any point in advance so that it is done and out of the way. Once the pork is almost cooked, add the half-and-half to the soup. Fill the soup plates and place them on the table. When the pork is done, remove it from the oven and cover it with foil. Then finish the sauce. You're now ready to sit down and enjoy the soup course. All you'll have to do is slice the pork and serve.

Chopped Winter Salad

Let these vegetable quantities be a rough guide. You can add more of any one you might like.

SALAD

4 cups shredded and chopped green cabbage

1 large red bell pepper, diced

2 small carrots, scraped and shredded

1 large bunch watercress, stems included, chopped coarsely

DRESSING

5 tablespoons olive oil

2 tablespoons balsamic vinegar

1 teaspoon salt

½ teaspoon black pepper

8 dashes Tabasco sauce

2 generous teaspoons ballpark (yellow) mustard

⅔ cup prepared mayonnaise

⅓ cup low-fat sour cream

2 generous tablespoons minced shallots

Make the salad. In a large bowl, combine the cabbage, red pepper, carrots, and watercress. Toss.

Make the dressing. In a small bowl, combine the oil, vinegar, salt, pepper, Tabasco sauce, and mustard and whisk until smooth. Add the mayonnaise and sour cream. Stir until smooth. Stir in the shallots.

Add about three-quarters of the dressing to the vegetables and toss. Add the balance if desired. I use it all, but some people like their salad less dressed.

Serves 6

LEFT: **The dressing ingredients for the Chopped Winter Salad.** OPPOSITE: **Toss the cabbage, red bell pepper, carrots, and watercress together by hand.**

Chocolate Toffee Nut Pudding Cake

This version of the old classic pudding cake came from my friend Laurie Wolf. You can serve this cake with Chocolate Whipped Cream (recipe follows), with vanilla ice cream, or plain. And it's equally good hot and at room temperature.

1 cup all-purpose flour
¾ cup granulated sugar
7 tablespoons unsweetened cocoa
2 teaspoons baking powder
¼ teaspoon salt
½ teaspoon instant espresso powder
1 teaspoon vanilla extract
½ cup milk
2 tablespoons canola oil
1 cup crushed Heath bars
1 cup chopped walnuts, plus additional for garnish
1 cup firmly packed light brown sugar
1¾ cups boiling water

Preheat the oven to 350 degrees and place a rack in the center of the oven. Generously butter a 1½-quart soufflé dish or a 9 × 9-inch pan.

In a large bowl, combine the flour, granulated sugar, 3 tablespoons of the cocoa, baking powder, salt, and espresso powder. Stir to mix well. Stir the vanilla into the milk. Add the milk and oil to the dry ingredients and mix well. Stir in the crushed Heath bars and nuts. The batter will be very stiff. Scrape it into the prepared dish with a rubber spatula.

In a small bowl, combine the brown sugar and remaining 4 tablespoons cocoa. Sprinkle this mixture over the top of the batter. Gently pour the boiling water over the batter—do not stir—and place in the preheated oven.

Bake 35 minutes, until the top looks crispy and cracked and a tester comes out clean when inserted into the "cake" part. Allow to rest a few minutes before serving with chocolate or plain whipped cream and chopped walnuts.

Serves 12

Chocolate Whipped Cream

This treat could also be great with plain angel cake.

1 ounce unsweetened chocolate
¼ cup sugar
1 cup plus 2 tablespoons heavy cream

Combine the chocolate, sugar, and 2 tablespoons of the cream in a small, heavy-bottomed saucepan. Place over low heat and stir until the chocolate is melted. Place the saucepan in a bowl of ice water and stir several times. Let the chocolate mixture cool.

In a medium bowl, whip the remaining cream until soft peaks form. Add the cooled chocolate mixture and whip to combine well.

Refrigerate, covered, until you're ready to serve it. Stir several times just before serving.

Makes about 2 cups

TOP: Just pour the boiling water over the batter; don't stir it in. ABOVE: The pudding cake is served in footed glass dishes, topped with the chocolate whipped cream and a sprinkling of chopped nuts.

Setting the Table

For a formal dinner at home, we set the table at a banquette off the kitchen, rather than in the dining room.

The place setting is a good example of mixing old and new. The underplate, dinner plate, and napkin are all new. The mismatched cutlery—the fork and bone-handled knife were found in England; the spoon has a mother-of-pearl handle—is all old. The wine glass is antique crystal. The round glass salt and pepper shakers are new.

No "centerpiece" here. Instead, the table was decorated with two topiary myrtle in clay pots. When not serving as a table decoration, these will grow nicely on a sunny windowsill. To keep them in shape, trim them with either gardening shears or a pair of sharp scissors.

Pork Medallions with Prunes and Port Sauce

You'll find this elegant little dish fast and easy.

1½ pounds pork loin, boned
Salt and black pepper to taste
All-purpose flour, for dredging
2 tablespoons (¼ stick) butter
1 cup chicken stock
1 cup port
12 pitted prunes, cut in half

Preheat the oven to its lowest setting (warm).

Cut the pork into 12 medallions. Season with salt and pepper and then dredge in flour, shaking off any excess (see the photograph above).

Heat the butter in a heavy skillet over medium-high heat and brown the meat 1 minute on each side, turning only once. Remove to a platter and keep warm in the oven.

Add the chicken stock and port to the pan and bring to a boil over medium heat, stirring to dissolve any brown bits in the pan. Add the prunes and increase the heat to high. Boil the sauce, stirring, until it coats the back of a spoon, 6 to 8 minutes.

Add the pork medallions to the sauce and cook for a minute or so, turning once to coat the meat.

Arrange 2 pork medallions on each plate and divide the sauce over each serving. Top each with 2 prune halves.

Serves 6

ABOVE, FROM LEFT: Pat any excess flour off the medallions. Turn the pork just once with tongs as you brown it. Let the pork cook with the prunes and sauce for a minute or two to combine the flavors.
RIGHT: Top each pork medallion with two prunes and a spoonful or so of the sauce.

New Potatoes Baked in Chicken Stock

Although these potatoes are best served about 10 minutes out of the oven, they can be reheated if necessary. They are even good the next day. Don't peel the potatoes—it's what makes them so good.

4 tablespoons (½ stick) unsalted butter

3 pounds new potatoes, well scrubbed and cut into ⅛-inch slices

¾ teaspoon salt

¼ teaspoon black pepper

3 large garlic cloves, peeled and minced

½ pound Emmentaler cheese, shredded

1⅓ cups chicken stock, heated

Preheat the oven to 375 degrees. Use 2 tablespoons of the butter to grease a 9 × 13-inch casserole. Place the sliced potatoes in cold water for about 30 minutes.

Drain the potatoes and dry them with paper towels. Place one-quarter of the potatoes in the casserole. Season with salt and pepper and sprinkle with one-third of the garlic and one-quarter of the cheese. Dot with butter. Make 3 more layers the same way (no garlic goes on top). Pour the stock over the potatoes. Bake for 1½ hours, covering loosely with foil for the last ¼ hour if the top is getting too browned. Allow to rest for about 10 minutes before serving.

Makes 6 generous servings

Grated Baked Beets

These beets reheat very well. For a change sometimes, pique their flavor with a tablespoon of fresh orange juice added with the butter.

10 medium beets

3 tablespoons unsalted butter

1 teaspoon salt

½ teaspoon black pepper

Preheat the oven to 400 degrees.

Wash the beets and trim off their tops, leaving the roots on. Place them in a foil-lined baking pan. Cover snugly with another sheet of foil and bake for 1½ hours, or until the beets can be easily pierced with a fork. When cool enough to handle, skin them (the skins will slip right off) and grate them coarsely. Toss with the other ingredients.

Makes 6 generous servings

SEAFOOD D

Growing up, I may not have known the pleasures of lobster thermidor or clams on the half shell, but that doesn't mean I didn't know the seductive flavors of seafood. After all, I had plump oysters, big blue crabs, and fat Gulf shrimp. Then there were the succulent freshwater shrimp and crawfish from slow-moving rivers and streams. You can bet we made the most of this abundance. This initiation had its effect on me, and I'm still likely to choose back fin lump crabmeat over lobster and gumbo over chowder.

So maybe it will come as no surprise that the first menu is centered around a mixed seafood ragout. It can be adapted to almost any combination of regularly available seafood, but I make sure it always has shrimp in it. This is traditionally served with rice, which I think makes for a pleasing mix of textures. You really don't need anything more than French bread and a salad with this, but I've given you a salad of mixed vegetables instead of greens. The dessert is a very light bread pudding gilded with chocolate sauce.

The main dish in the second menu—a seafood Creole—has been one of my favorites since I was a kid. In our house it was usually prepared with shrimp and crawfish but sometimes it even had crabmeat added to it.

These meals were planned for six to eight.

INNERS

Mixed Seafood Ragout

We made this with five different kinds of seafood, but you can certainly add or subtract from the list as long as you wind up with roughly the same total amount of seafood.

If you don't have the amount of oyster liquid called for in the recipe, make up the difference with more bottled clam juice—or use all clam juice.

6 tablespoons (¾ stick) unsalted butter
1 large garlic clove
1 cup minced celery
1 cup minced green bell pepper
1 cup minced yellow onion
7 tablespoons all-purpose flour
½ cup oyster liquor
1 8-ounce bottle clam juice
1 14-ounce can low-salt chicken broth
1½ cups water
1 large bay leaf
½ teaspoon black pepper
, ½ teaspoon salt
¼ pound deveined and peeled shrimp
¼ pound lobster meat (from a 1½-pound lobster—see Note)
¼ pound sea scallops, cut in half
1 pint crabmeat, picked over
1 pint shucked oysters, drained
¼ teaspoon Tabasco sauce

Melt 5 tablespoons of the butter in a large, heavy skillet over medium heat. Add the garlic, celery, bell pepper, and onion and cook until wilted but not browned, about 10 minutes. Sprinkle 5 tablespoons of flour over the vegetables and cook, stirring, for 5 minutes. Combine the oyster liquor, clam juice, chicken broth, and water in a pitcher. Add the liquids gradually to the vegetables in the skillet, stirring to incorporate. Add the bay leaf, pepper, and salt. Cook over very low heat, stirring occasionally, about 1 hour, until reduced. (The dish can be prepared in advance up to this point.)

Mash the remaining tablespoon of butter with the 2 remaining tablespoons of flour.

To complete the dish, raise the heat to medium-high and whisk in the butter–flour mixture a little at a time. Simmer until thickened, about 5 minutes. Stir in the seafood. Cook 5 minutes, or until the shrimp are just pink. Do not overcook. Stir in the Tabasco sauce.

Serves 6 to 8

NOTE: You don't want fully cooked lobster here, but you should cook it a bit to make it easier to get out of the shell. This is what to do: Bring a large pot of water to a full boil. Plunge the lobster in headfirst and cover the pot. Cook for 3 or 4 minutes, just until the shell turns red. Remove the lobster from the pot and let it cool. When it's cool enough to handle, crack the shell and pull the meat from the tail and claws. Cut the lobster into chunks.

PRECEDING PAGES: Stir the seafood into the sauce gently. Use a wooden spoon and try not to break up the crabmeat.
OPPOSITE: Put the Boiled Rice on the plate and make a well in the center; fill it with the Mixed Seafood Ragout, and garnish with a sprig of flat-leafed parsley.

Boiled Rice

To add a little extra flavor to the rice you might cook it in chicken stock.

1 cup long-grain white rice
5 cups cold water
1 tablespoon salt

Combine all the ingredients in a deep saucepan. Bring to a boil, uncovered, over medium-high heat. Turn the heat down so the rice cooks at a slow, rolling boil. Test for doneness after 10 minutes. Drain in a colander and wash briefly with hot water. Fluff with a fork.

Serves 6 to 8

VARIATION

Buttered Rice with Parsley

Prepare the recipe as above. When you fluff the rice, stir in 1 tablespoon softened butter and 2 tablespoons minced fresh parsley.

Vegetable Salad

Feel free to add any other vegetable you like, but blanch any fibrous ones.

1 cup julienne carrots
1 cup string beans, tips and strings removed
1 cup wax beans, tips and strings removed
¼ cup green onions, with some green, cut into small rings
½ cup small yellow squash, cut into small rings
1 medium red bell pepper, roasted and cut into ¼-inch strips (see Note)
3 tablespoons olive oil
1 tablespoon white wine vinegar
½ teaspoon salt
¼ teaspoon pepper
¼ cup chopped fresh dill (no stems)

Bring a medium saucepan of water to a boil over medium-high heat.

Add the carrots and cook for 6 minutes, until just barely tender. Take the carrots out with a skimmer and place in a bowl of ice water to stop the cooking. Add the string and wax beans to the water and cook for 10 minutes, until just barely tender. Drain and place the beans in the ice water with the carrots. When the vegetables are cool, drain them well and dry them with paper towels.

Place the blanched vegetables in a large bowl with the green onions, squash, and roasted pepper. Toss.

In a small bowl, whisk together the olive oil, vinegar, salt, and pepper. Stir in the dill and pour over the vegetables. Toss.

Serves 6

NOTE: Here's my simple method for roasting peppers. Place 1 or 2 bell peppers on a foil-lined baking sheet and place under a preheated broiler. Turn them carefully with tongs from time to time until the skin is black and charred all over. Take them off the baking sheet and place in a small paper bag. Fold the bag shut and let sit for 15 to 20 minutes. Remove and discard the skin, core, and pits.

OPPOSITE: The tossed Vegetable Salad is a good change from the standard green salad.

Start this menu the night
before by slicing and trim-
ming the bread for the
pudding. Let the bread sit
out uncovered overnight.
On the morning or early
afternoon of your dinner,
make the bread pudding,
and while it's baking,
make the chocolate sauce.
This can be left at room
temperature and stirred
once you are ready to
serve it.

Now get started on the
seafood ragout. Cleaning
the seafood will take some
time, so precook the lob-
ster, peel and devein the
shrimp, cut the scallops,
and pick over the crab-
meat. Keep this very cold
in the refrigerator. Then
prepare the ragout sauce
and let it reduce.

While the ragout is
reducing, prepare the vegetables for the salad.
Combine the vegetables,
but don't add the dressing.

When your guests
arrive, it's an easy job to
cook the rice, finish the
ragout, and dress the
salad.

Light Bread Pudding with Chocolate Sauce

Using low-fat milk in place of the more traditional cream gives this version of the old standby a distinctly lighter texture and taste.

BREAD PUDDING

8 tablespoons (1 stick) unsalted butter, softened
10 or more 1-inch slices day-old French bread, crusts trimmed
2 whole eggs
2 portions egg substitute
¾ cup plus 2 tablespoons sugar
4 cups low-fat milk
2 tablespoons vanilla extract
Freshly grated nutmeg

CHOCOLATE SAUCE

1 cup heavy cream
4 ounces bittersweet chocolate, coarsely chopped

Preheat the oven to 350 degrees.

Make the bread pudding. Grease a 2-quart ovenproof casserole with some of the butter. Spread the remaining butter on one side of the bread slices. Place the bread, buttered side up, in a single layer in the casserole.

In a medium bowl, beat the eggs, egg substitute, and ¾ cup of the sugar together. Stir in the milk, vanilla extract, and a few grinds of nutmeg.

Pour the mixture carefully through a strainer into the casserole. The bread will float to the top. Sprinkle the top with the 2 additional tablespoons of sugar. Put the casserole in a larger ovenproof pan and surround with enough boiling water to come ½ inch up the sides of the casserole. Put the pan in the center of the oven and reduce the heat to 325 degrees. Bake for 45 minutes, or until a knife inserted in the bread pudding comes out clean. This may still seem a little soft but will set as it cools. Allow to cool completely, then refrigerate, covered.

Make the chocolate sauce. Heat the cream in a small, heavy-bottomed saucepan—do not let it boil. Remove from the heat and add the chocolate; stir until melted and smooth. Set aside, covered, at room temperature.

Serve in dessert bowls with some chocolate sauce spooned on top.

Serves 8

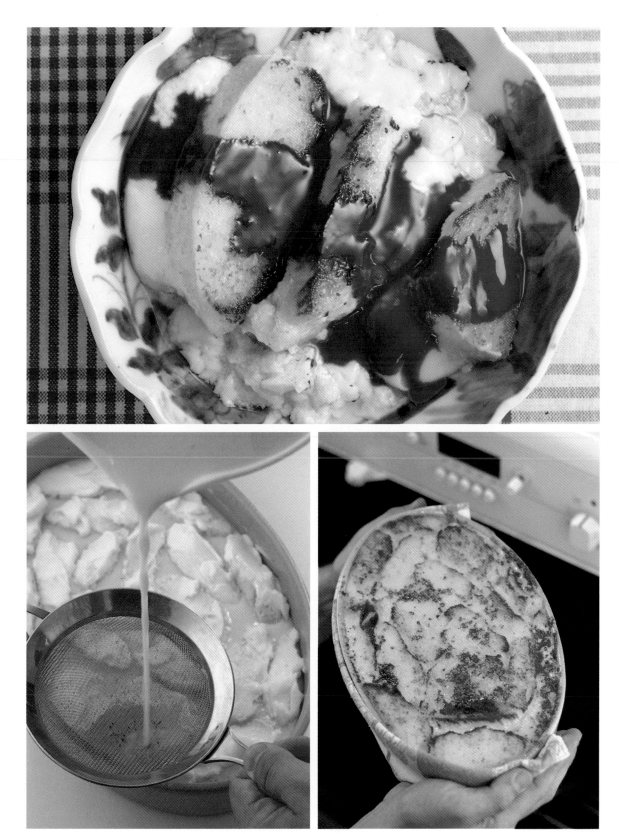

TOP: The Light Bread Pudding is served topped with Chocolate Sauce. ABOVE LEFT: Pour the custard mixture over the bread through a fine sieve. ABOVE RIGHT: When done, the bread pudding will be nicely browned.

Setting the Table

Here you find a comfortable table with a Japanese theme set in a Long Island dining room.

With the table covered by a blue-and-white plaid linen cloth, repeating the ticking on the seats of the wicker chairs, it seemed the ideal choice was white cotton napkins. The dinner plates are contemporary Japanese, while the bowls used for the vegetable salad and the bread pudding are vintage blue-and-white porcelain. The flatware has boxwood handles, and the wine glasses are simple clear glass, as are the low candlesticks.

Again, garden flowers are used for the centerpiece. We chose perfect specimens of different flowers—hydrangeas, roses, and sunflowers—and cut the stems to fit the old frosted glass containers.

New Orleans Shrimp and Crawfish Creole

The reason shrimp Creole has endured so long is that it is so simple to make—and delicious, a hard-to-beat combo. As you can imagine, there are dozens of recipes for this New Orleans classic. This one is based on a recipe from Commander's Palace restaurant.

2 tablespoons margarine
1 cup minced onion
1 cup minced green bell pepper
2 celery ribs, minced
2 large garlic cloves, peeled and thinly sliced
1 bay leaf
2 tablespoons paprika
2 cups peeled, seeded, and diced tomatoes (or an equal amount of drained canned tomatoes)
1 cup thick tomato juice
4 teaspoons Worcestershire sauce
4 teaspoons Louisiana Hot Sauce (or Tabasco sauce)
1½ tablespoons cornstarch
½ cup cold water
3 tablespoons unsalted butter
1½ pounds peeled, deveined shrimp
1½ pounds peeled crawfish tails (may use frozen)

In a large skillet, melt the margarine over a medium flame. Add the onion, bell pepper, celery, and garlic and cook for a minute or two, until wilted. Add the bay leaf, paprika, tomatoes, and tomato juice. Stir well and add the Worcestershire and hot sauce. Stir again and simmer over medium-low heat until reduced by a quarter, about 30 minutes.

Mix the cornstarch and water together to dissolve any lumps and stir into the sauce. Cook, stirring, for about 2 minutes to thicken the sauce slightly.

Melt the butter in a large skillet over medium-high heat. Add the shrimp and crawfish and cook, tossing, until pink, about 5 minutes. If your crawfish is already cooked, add it once the shrimp is done and just heat it through. Add the seafood to the sauce and cook for a minute.

Serve over rice.

Serves 6 to 8

TOP: The shrimp should be cooked in the sauce just until they're pink. ABOVE: As with the ragout, make a bed of boiled rice and spoon the New Orleans Shrimp and Crawfish Creole over it. Garnish with a large sprig of flat-leafed parsley.

SOUP DINN

Anumber of years ago I realized I was serving soup as a main course for little dinners and people really seemed to enjoy it. The upshot of this was a book called *Soup Meals.* Anyway, I still think building a meal around soup is a terrific idea, as well as being popular with guests.

Obviously this concept could go in many directions, depending on your personal soup preferences and how much time you have to spend on it.

The two soups featured here are a delectable bean and pasta combination and a soup made from leafy greens and potatoes. Both have a second course of a composed salad that includes roasted onions piqued with balsamic vinegar, steamed asparagus, boiled new potatoes, roasted red peppers, and hard-cooked eggs, all served with a nice strong vinaigrette.

Incidentally, this salad is very flexible. You can use any vegetables that you might like, and you can dress it up by adding cured meats and fish. These salads are best served at room temperature. Don't refrigerate them unless you've cooked the ingredients far in advance, and if you do refrigerate, make sure you let the salad come back to room temperature before you serve it.

Dessert is an old family favorite: burnt sugar pecan cake. You could obviously gild the lily by adding whipped cream or ice cream—choose your poison.

Soup dinners for six.

ERS

Pasta and Bean Soup

There is a very simple way to alter the flavor of this soup. The recipe calls for crushed tomatoes, which are available with and without tomato paste added. If you use the one without paste, the tomato flavor is a bit more subtle; with the paste the flavor is more pronounced. Good both ways. Incidentally, the soup in the photograph was made using the crushed tomatoes with paste.

¼ pound thick-sliced bacon
5 tablespoons olive oil
½ cup minced onion
½ cup minced celery
½ cup minced carrot
1½ cups canned crushed tomatoes
2 19-ounce cans cannellini beans, drained
8 cups chicken stock
1 teaspoon salt
½ teaspoon black pepper
1 cup small elbow macaroni

Bring a small saucepan of water to a simmer. Cut the bacon strips into 4 equal pieces each, add to the water, and blanch for 5 minutes. Drain, dry the bacon well, and fry until crisp. Set the bacon aside and reserve 2 tablespoons of the bacon fat.

Heat the bacon fat and the olive oil in a stockpot over medium heat. Add the onion, celery, and carrot. Cover and cook, stirring occasionally, until the vegetables begin to brown, about 10 minutes. Add the tomatoes and increase the heat to high. Cook, stirring, until reduced and slightly darkened, about 8 minutes (see the photograph below). Add the beans, stock, salt, and pepper. Bring to a boil, then turn back to a simmer. Cook 5 minutes. Use the back of a spoon to mash some of the beans (this will thicken the soup slightly). You can prepare the recipe up to this point in advance. Set it aside, covered.

Add the reserved bacon and the macaroni. Bring back to a boil and cook for 5 minutes. Cover the pot and remove it from the heat. Allow to rest 5 minutes before serving. Serve immediately.

Serves 6

PRECEDING PAGES: **A basket of bread and crusty rolls, with sweet butter, is a natural go-along for a soup dinner.** RIGHT: **Cook the aromatics and tomatoes for the soup until reduced and slightly darkened.** OPPOSITE: **Ladle out the Pasta and Bean Soup at the table.** OVERLEAF: **The Composed Salad.**

Composed Salad

Feel free to delete from or add to the list of vegetables below.

SALAD

    1 large onion

    1 teaspoon olive oil

    1 teaspoon balsamic vinegar

    Salt and black pepper to taste

    18 medium to large asparagus, woody ends snapped off

    12 small red potatoes

VINAIGRETTE

    4 tablespoons olive oil

    2 tablespoons canola oil

    ¾ teaspoon salt

    ½ teaspoon pepper

    1 generous teaspoon green peppercorn mustard (Dijon can be substituted)

    2 tablespoons balsamic vinegar

    Lettuce leaves for garnish (optional)

    1 large red bell pepper, roasted and cut into strips (see Note, page 89)

    6 hard-cooked eggs, peeled and halved

    Roughly grated Parmesan cheese

Preheat the oven to 350 degrees.

Make the salad. Peel the onion and cut it through, top to root end, into 6 wedges. Tear off a square of foil and stand the cut onion in the center. Spoon the olive oil and balsamic vinegar over it and sprinkle with salt and pepper. Bring the corners of the foil up and twist to close, pressing the foil against the onion. Place on a small pan and bake for 1 hour and 20 minutes, until tender. Open the foil pack to let the onion cool.

Bring a skillet of salted water to a boil. Add the asparagus and cook over medium-low heat for 4 or 5 minutes, until just barely tender. Drain and immediately run under cool water to stop the cooking. Pat dry and set aside. If not using right away, wrap the cooled asparagus in damp paper towels.

Scrub the potatoes and cut each in quarters. Place in a saucepan and cover with cold water. Add salt to taste. Bring to a boil over high heat. Turn the heat down and cook at a slow boil for about 10 minutes, until tender. Drain the potatoes, rinse them in cold water, pat them dry, and set aside.

Make the vinaigrette. Combine all the ingredients in a jar with a tight-fitting lid and shake briskly. Set aside at room temperature for up to 3 hours.

Compose the salad. Have all ingredients at room temperature. Place a small, crisp lettuce leaf on a luncheon or dinner plate. Top this with 3 asparagus spears. Place a wide strip of roasted pepper over the asparagus. Surround the asparagus with a wedge of onion, some potatoes, and 2 egg halves (see the photograph). Sprinkle the whole plate with the roughly grated Parmesan. Spoon a little vinaigrette over each serving.

Serves 6

ABOVE: Rather than whisking the vinaigrette, put the ingredients in a jar with a tight cover and shake vigorously.

Seafood Composed Salad

Prepare the recipe as above. Bring a medium pan of salted water to a boil. Add 18 large shrimp (in their shells) to the water and boil until pink and cooked through. Drain the shrimp, peel them, and add them to the plate.

CLOCKWISE, FROM TOP LEFT: The potatoes are covered with well-salted water for cooking. Wrap the quartered onion in foil before baking. Refresh the cooked asparagus under cold water to stop the cooking. Arrange each element of the Composed Salad carefully on the plate.

The best place to start is
with the dessert. Make the
cake and set it aside to
cool before you make the
frosting. The cake can be
frosted at any time once it
has cooled.

While the cake is in the
oven, you can organize the
elements for the composed
salad. Except for the onion
and pepper, the vegeta-
bles for the salad are done
on top of the stove.

Have the onion ready to
roast as soon as you take
the cake out. Cook and
peel the eggs. Prepare the
vinaigrette.

The basic preparation
for the soup can be done
ahead of time. After you
mash the beans into the
soup, cover it and set
aside.

Next assemble the com-
posed salads. Arrange
them on appropriate
plates and keep them at
room temperature. Dress
them just before serving. (I
am assuming that the
salad will not be sitting
out for more than 30 or 40
minutes.)

The last thing you'll
need to do is bring the
soup back to heat, add the
bacon and macaroni, and
finish the cooking—which
will take about 15 minutes.

Burnt Sugar Pecan Cake with Caramel Icing

A version of this cake was a great family favorite of ours. Taste it and you'll know why. Incidentally, you can make just the icing, pour it into an oiled pan, and let it set. Cut it into squares and serve it as candy.

CAKE

1½ cups sugar

¾ cup boiling water

1½ cups pecans, toasted and coarsely chopped (see Note)

2½ cups all-purpose flour

1 teaspoon baking powder

¾ teaspoon baking soda

12 tablespoons (1½ sticks) unsalted butter, softened

2 eggs, separated

1 cup milk

Pinch of salt

1 teaspoon vanilla extract

Caramel Icing (recipe follows)

Make the cake. Place ½ cup plus 2 tablespoons of the sugar in a medium saucepan over medium heat. Cook, without stirring, until the sugar is melted and a dark caramel color, 7 to 10 minutes. Remove from the heat and carefully add the boiling water—this will spatter, so be careful. Return to the heat and cook, stirring, for a minute or so until the caramel is melted and the syrup is smooth. Set aside to cool.

Preheat the oven to 350 degrees. Grease and lightly flour two 9-inch round cake pans.

In a small bowl, toss the pecans with ½ cup of the flour. Place the remaining flour in another bowl, add the baking powder and baking soda, and stir.

In a large bowl, cream the butter and the remaining sugar until light and fluffy. Beat the egg yolks lightly. Add the sugar syrup to the yolks and mix. Stir this into the butter mixture and beat well. Add the dry ingredients, alternating with the milk, beginning and ending with the dry. Fold the pecans and what-ever flour remains into the batter.

Beat the egg whites with the salt until stiff but not dry. Gently fold the whites and the vanilla into the batter. Pour into the prepared pans. Bake until golden and a cake tester comes out clean, about 25 minutes. Allow to cool slightly on racks, then remove from the pans. Allow to cool completely.

Brush the crumbs off the cake layers. Place one layer on a cake plate and pour half the frosting onto it. Working quickly, allow the icing to flow over the sides naturally. Dip a spatula in hot water and use it to smooth the top of the icing. Add the second layer and hold it in place with toothpicks if necessary. Pour the remaining icing over the top layer, again allowing it to drip down the sides.

Serves 12

OPPOSITE: **Allow the
Caramel Icing to drip
down the sides of the
Burnt Sugar Pecan
Cake naturally.**

NOTE: To toast the pecans, place the nuts in an ovenproof skillet and bake in a preheated 350-degree oven for 10 to 15 minutes, shaking the skillet from time to time, until the nuts are fragrant and lightly browned.

Caramel Icing

Be sure you have a little extra heavy cream on hand in case the icing needs thinning—it often does.

BELOW: The sugars,
cream, and butter have
been cooked to the soft
ball stage. BOTTOM: If the
icing is too thick to pour,
thin it with a bit more
heavy cream. OPPOSITE:
You can garnish the
Pureed Broccoli Rabe
Soup with a pinch of
fresh herbs.

2 cups firmly packed dark brown sugar
½ cup granulated sugar
1 cup heavy cream
4 tablespoons (½ stick) unsalted butter
1 tablespoon vanilla extract
1½ cups pecans, toasted and coarsely chopped (see Note, page 104)

Place all ingredients except the vanilla and pecans in a heavy saucepan over low heat. Cook until the butter is melted. Increase the heat to medium and continue to boil, stirring, until the soft ball stage (235 degrees on a candy thermometer). Allow to cool for 5 to 10 minutes.

Stir in the vanilla. Beat at high speed with an electric hand mixer until it is almost spreading consistency. Quickly stir in the pecans. If it thickens too much, add a bit more heavy cream.

Makes enough for two 9-inch layers

Menu II

Pureed Broccoli Rabe
Soup
(page 107)

Bread and Rolls

Seafood Composed
Salad
(page 103)

Lemon Pudding Cake
(page 53)

Pureed Broccoli Rabe Soup

¼ cup olive oil
1 pound broccoli rabe, stems trimmed, coarsely chopped
7¼ cups chicken stock
1 large onion, diced
2 large carrots, scraped and diced
2 celery ribs, diced
1 cup water
2 small baking potatoes, peeled and diced
2 garlic cloves, minced
½ teaspoon salt
¼ teaspoon black pepper

Put 2 tablespoons of the olive oil in a deep pot over high heat. Wash the chopped broccoli rabe and add it to the oil with any water clinging to it. Toss and add ¼ cup of the chicken stock. Reduce the heat to medium, cover, and cook until tender, about 15 minutes.

Meanwhile, put the remaining 2 tablespoons of olive oil in another pot over medium heat and add the onion, carrots, and celery. Cook until wilted, about 5 minutes. Add the remaining 7 cups stock, the water, potatoes, and garlic. Bring to a boil over high heat. Turn back to a slow boil and cook until the potatoes are soft, about 15 minutes. Add the broccoli rabe and mix. Cook for 5 minutes to blend the flavors.

Allow the soup to cool slightly, then puree in the food processor or put through a food mill. Season with the salt and pepper.

Serves 6

Setting the Table

Here's a comfortable, casual table in a New York City loft—another mix of old and new.

Paper doilies have been used as placemats. The underplate is a restaurant charger, the dinner plate is the "Davenport" pattern, and the silverplate flatware is called "Baguette." All are combined with a cotton napkin having a grapevine pattern. The wine glasses and pitcher are old; the tureen is a new piece from Leedsware, and we used an oval restaurant plate as a butter dish.

For the centerpiece, we bought blooming ranunculus and replanted them in antique celadon cachepots. We added an old three-armed candelabrum with ivy—planted in a simple terra-cotta container—clinging to its arms. The ivy sits in a sunny window when not in use on the table.

VEGETARIA

When I was growing up our family had all-vegetable dinners at least once a week. During their seasons there would be tomatoes fresh from the vine, English peas, carrots, green onions, greens of all kinds, field peas, cow peas, lady peas, butter beans, snap beans, lima beans, beets, okra, squash of every kind—the sweetest came in the fall—corn, eggplant, new and sweet potatoes. This tradition held right until the first frost when root vegetables were gathered and stored. What I didn't know then was that these were vegetarian dinners. So I guess I've been part vegetarian all my life without quite realizing it—but enjoying it.

The two dinners here—one based on an old family favorite, stuffed cabbage, and another built around chef Michael Romano's great crustless vegetable tart—are both treats for the eyes as well as the palate.

The first is the more elaborate and a natural centerpiece for a big meal: a whole head of cabbage, stuffed with rice, pasta, bulgur, and other good things.

To begin there's a wonderfully fresh-tasting uncooked tomato soup, which is served either chilled or at room temperature accompanied by crisp "cracker" bread. After all that, I figured a simple dessert of fruit and cookies would be welcome.

The second menu is probably best for a light supper—but it could certainly be made more important and substantial by adding another course or two. You might start with the tomato soup and add the baked new potatoes and grated beets.

These will serve six to eight.

N DINNERS

Uncooked Tomato Soup

You could stir a bit of crabmeat or some small boiled shrimp into this soup and
make a meal of it.

SOUP

3 pounds tomatoes, peeled, seeded, and chopped
1 green bell pepper, seeded and coarsely chopped
1 small cucumber, peeled, seeded, and coarsely chopped
3 celery ribs, peeled
2 tablespoons olive oil
¼ cup tarragon vinegar
10 small basil leaves, coarsely chopped
1 tablespoon chopped fresh tarragon leaves
1 cup vegetable stock
Salt and black pepper to taste

OPTIONAL GARNISH

Yogurt or crème fraîche (optional)
Chopped fresh herbs (optional)

Put all the soup ingredients but the stock, salt, and pepper in a food processor or
blender and process to a rough texture. Pour into a large bowl and stir in the
stock. Taste for salt and pepper. If the soup is too thick, thin with a little extra
stock.

Chill the soup for at least half an hour before serving. Garnish with a dollop
of yogurt and some chopped herbs if you care to. (See photograph on pages
110–111.)

Serves 8 or more

PRECEDING PAGES: **The
Uncooked Tomato Soup
is garnished with a
dollop of yogurt and
snipped chives.** RIGHT:
**You can puree the soup
in a blender.**

Cracker Bread

I think you'll be pleasantly surprised at how easy this is to make.

3 tablespoons shelled sunflower seeds
1¼ cups all-purpose flour
¾ teaspoon sugar
¾ teaspoon baking powder
¼ teaspoon baking soda
½ teaspoon salt
6 tablespoons grated Parmesan cheese
2 tablespoons (¼ stick) cold unsalted butter, cut into small pieces
½ cup buttermilk
Coarse salt

Preheat the oven to 425 degrees. Lightly oil the backs of three baking sheets.

In a bowl, mix the seeds, flour, sugar, baking power, baking soda, salt, and 3 tablespoons of the Parmesan. Add the butter and mix with your fingers until the mixture is mealy. Stir in the buttermilk quickly. The dough should be moist but not sticky. (If it is sticky, knead in a little more flour briefly.)

Divide the dough into 3 balls. Place one in the center of one of the greased baking sheets. Roll out paper-thin, literally. Sprinkle with a tablespoon of the reserved Parmesan and press the cheese into the surface of the dough. Cut into large cracker shapes or strips with a pizza cutter or a knife (see the photograph below left). Be careful; if you drag the tip of a knife over the dough to cut it, the dough will snag and wrinkle in spots. Slightly separate the crackers on the sheet. Prick with the tines of a fork and sprinkle with coarse salt. Repeat with the other two-thirds of the dough.

Bake until golden, about 8 minutes. Cool on a rack.

Makes about 48 crackers

BELOW: Use a sharp pizza cutter to slice the rolled-out cracker dough. RIGHT: The Cracker Bread is very crisp and very easy to make. OVERLEAF: The platter of stuffed cabbage is garnished with steamed cabbage and slices of Baked Acorn Squash.

Cabbage Stuffed with Grain, Pasta, Nuts, and Vegetables

Not only is this very tasty, it makes a very pretty presentation. However, if you want, you might just bake the stuffing in a casserole and serve it with a simple tomato sauce.

1 large head of green cabbage
3 tablespoons olive oil
1 cup chopped onion
2 cups thickly sliced white mushrooms
½ cup minced celery
¾ cup minced red bell pepper
1 large garlic clove, finely chopped
½ cup shredded carrot
½ finely sliced green onion, with some green
2 tablespoons minced parsley
½ cup coarsely chopped toasted pecans (or hazelnuts) (see Note, page 104)
¾ teaspoon salt
¼ teaspoon black pepper
¼ teaspoon dried thyme
Pinch of cayenne pepper
6½ cups chicken stock
½ cup bulgur wheat
½ cup *acini di pepe* pasta (or other very small soup pasta)
½ cup long-grain white rice

GARNISH

2 tablespoons (¼ stick) butter
4½ teaspoons rice wine vinegar
Salt and pepper to taste

Peel several outer leaves from the cabbage head and set aside. (These will be used to decorate the dish when it is served.) Cut off the core end of the cabbage. Remove the core without disturbing the outer walls and discard. Using a small pointed paring knife and making short, slashing, crosshatch motions, hollow out the entire cabbage head, leaving about a ¾-inch outer wall intact (see the photograph). Reserve both the cabbage shell and the chopped cabbage.

Heat a tablespoon of the oil in a heavy skillet over medium-high heat. Add

RIGHT: Here, the nuts and vegetables for the stuffing are ready for tossing. FAR RIGHT: The completed stuffing is ready to go into the cabbage.

the onion and cook until golden, about 10 minutes. Set aside in a large bowl. Add another tablespoon of the oil to the skillet and sauté the mushrooms over high heat until browned, about 4 minutes. Add to the bowl with the onion. Add the last tablespoon of oil to the skillet and sauté the celery and pepper over medium-high heat for a minute. Add the garlic and cook another minute. Set aside in the bowl with the other vegetables.

Toss the carrot, green onion, parsley, and pecans with the cooked vegetables. Sprinkle with the salt, pepper, thyme, and cayenne. Toss to mix. Stir in ½ cup of the chicken stock. Set aside.

Heat the remaining stock in a deep saucepan over high heat. When boiling, add the bulgur, pasta, and rice. Bring back to a boil. When boiling, turn the heat back to medium and cook until almost tender, about 10 minutes. Drain and discard any remaining stock. Add the pasta and grains to the other ingredients. Toss to mix well.

Spread a 4-foot length of doubled cheesecloth on the counter. Place the cabbage, open side up, in the center. Spoon the stuffing mixture into the cavity, pressing down lightly. When the cabbage is full, pile the rest on top, pressing down gently to make a mound. Gather the ends of the cheesecloth together and tie it shut around the stuffed cabbage.

Put 2 inches of water in a large pot and bring to a boil over high heat. Insert a steamer (I use a pasta pot with a perforated insert for this). Add the cabbage, cover, and steam until the cabbage is tender, about 1 hour. Be sure to check the water from time to time so it doesn't boil away.

Make the garnish. Bring an inch of water to a boil in a saucepan. Insert a steamer, add the reserved chopped cabbage, and steam for about 4 minutes, until tender. Season with the butter, rice wine vinegar, salt, and pepper.

To serve, make a bed of steamed chopped cabbage on a platter. Top with the stuffed cabbage and the reserved outer leaves. Cut into wedges and mound each serving with the stuffing.

Serves 8

FROM LEFT: **Make crosshatches with a sharp knife to hollow out the cabbage. Mound the cabbage high with the stuffing and tie it up with cheesecloth. Leave a "tail" of cheesecloth so you can lower the cabbage into the pot.**

Start with the soup. Peel and seed the vegetables, then puree the soup and set it aside to chill.

Next should be the cracker bread. The finished crackers can be stored quite successfully in an airtight metal tin or plastic container.

Now mix and bake those wonderful chocolate cookies. These too can be stored in an airtight metal tin or plastic container. While they are baking, prepare the fruit for the salad. The grapes should be cut in half, the melon cubed, and the blueberries picked over, and the pith removed from the oranges.

Next, get the stuffed cabbage ready for baking. Chop the vegetables and core the cabbage. Put the stock for the grain and pasta on to heat while you sauté the vegetables. Stuff the cabbage and tie it in cheesecloth.

Now get the squash ready to go into the oven. Begin baking the squash at the same time you start steaming the cabbage—both will take about an hour to cook. Then all that's left to do is to quickly steam the chopped cabbage. Add the banana to the fruit just before serving.

Baked Acorn Squash

These may be cooked either in a conventional oven or in a microwave oven—which is, of course, quicker.

4 medium acorn squash, halved lengthwise and seeded
4 tablespoons (½ stick) unsalted butter
Salt and black pepper to taste

Preheat the oven to 350 degrees.

Place the squash halves, cut sides down, on a lightly greased baking sheet. Bake for 30 minutes. Turn over, dot with butter, and sprinkle with salt and pepper. Bake another 30 minutes, until fork-tender.

To cook in the microwave, place the squash halves in a covered dish and dot with the butter. Season with salt and pepper to taste. Cover. Microwave on HIGH until tender, about 18 minutes.

To serve, cut each half in 2 crosswise.

Serves 8

Mixed Fruit Cup

You can make this in advance, but don't add the banana until just before serving.

2 large seedless oranges, peeled (see Note)
¾ cup red seedless grapes, cut in half
1 cup blueberries
1 small honeydew melon, seeded, peeled, and cut into medium cubes
1 large ripe banana, cut into rings
Sugar to taste
½ cup freshly squeezed orange juice

Cut the oranges crosswise into 6 slices, then cut each of them in quarters. Place in a glass bowl with the other fruit. Sprinkle with sugar and toss with the orange juice. Serve in small bowls or cups.

Serves 8

NOTE: It is very important to get rid of the white pith after the oranges are peeled. If it is difficult to remove, drop the peeled oranges very briefly (about 5 seconds) into boiling water. The pith should then be easier to scrape off.

TOP: Giving a peeled orange a quick bath in boiling water will make it easier to remove all traces of pith. ABOVE: You can use two spoons (or your hands) to toss the fruit.

Dropped Brownie Cookies

The little bit of pepper here adds zip. I'm sure you can imagine how good these would be with a glass of cold milk or ice cream.

4 ounces semisweet chocolate
1 ounce unsweetened chocolate
8 tablespoons (1 stick) unsalted butter
1 cup sugar
1 teaspoon vanilla extract
½ teaspoon salt
½ teaspoon black pepper
2 eggs, lightly beaten
1½ cups all-purpose flour
1 teaspoon baking powder
1¾ cups chopped toasted walnuts (see Note, page 104)

Preheat the oven to 350 degrees.

Combine the semisweet and unsweetened chocolate with the butter in a small saucepan and melt over medium-low heat. Remove from the heat and transfer to a mixing bowl. Add the sugar, vanilla, salt, and pepper. Mix well and allow to cool slightly. Stir in the eggs. Combine the flour and baking powder and stir into the mixture. Then stir in the nuts.

Drop by rounded teaspoons onto an ungreased cookie sheet.

Bake for 12 minutes. Allow to cool for a few minutes before removing to a rack to cool completely.

Makes 30 or more

TOP: Push the rounded spoonfuls of cookie dough off onto the baking sheet with your finger. ABOVE: The Dropped Brownie Cookies should cool completely on a rack.

Setting the Table

Here you have a simple but elegant table, set out on the porch of an East Hampton house.

Rather than arranging flowers for the table, we used a collection of ceramic red peppers on a plain white plate. The candelabra are old metal pieces from France. This effect could be approximated by wiring pearl drops to a multi-armed candelabrum from a flea market or yard sale.

The place setting is composed of old and new pieces. The underplate is "White Crackle" from Molin; the dinner plate is a Japanese "swirl" plate; the top plate (the liner for the clear glass soup bowl) is vintage Japanese porcelain. The flatware has wooden handles, and the napkins are hemstitched linen.

Eggplant, Zucchini, and Parmesan Tortino

A tortino is a crustless pie or tart. This recipe was inspired by one from Michael Romano of the Union Square Cafe in New York City. I've reduced the fat in my version. Incidentally, this can be made the day before and reheated. It also makes a delicious main course with a light tomato sauce.

> ¾ cup plus one tablespoon olive oil
> 1 pound Spanish onions, cut into ¼-inch slices
> Salt and black pepper to taste
> 1 pound eggplant, peeled, quartered lengthwise, and cut into ¼-inch slices
> ½ pound zucchini, washed and sliced into ¼-inch rounds
> ½ pound yellow squash, washed and sliced into ¼-inch rounds
> 2 whole eggs
> 3 portions egg substitute
> 2 tablespoons balsamic vinegar
> 1 cup evaporated skim milk
> ½ cup grated Parmesan cheese

Preheat the oven to 325 degrees.

Heat ¼ cup of the olive oil in a large skillet over medium-high heat. Add the onions and cook until tender, about 5 to 6 minutes. Season with salt and pepper and put into a large mixing bowl.

Using another ¼ cup of the olive oil, sauté the eggplant, zucchini, and yellow squash over high heat until tender, 6 to 8 minutes. Add to the onions.

In a medium bowl, whisk together the eggs, egg substitute, ¼ cup of olive oil, the vinegar, evaporated skim milk, and ¼ cup of Parmesan. Pour this over the vegetables and mix gently.

Use 1 tablespoon of olive oil to grease a 2-inch-deep 2-quart square baking dish. Pour in the vegetable mixture. Cover with foil and bake for 45 minutes. Remove the foil and sprinkle with the remaining Parmesan. Bake for an additional 15 minutes. Run under the broiler briefly to brown lightly. Allow to rest at least an hour before slicing into squares.

Before serving, reheat in the oven or under the broiler.

Serves 6

ABOVE: The Eggplant, Zucchini, and Parmesan Tortino is cut into squares for serving.

UNLESS OTHERWISE SPECIFIED, ITEMS IN
THE PHOTOGRAPHS ARE IN PRIVATE COLLECTIONS.

Beef Dinners

The dinner fork and knife are
Christofle's "Albi." The red wine glass
is Baccarat's "Paris."

Casserole Dinners

Libby's "Gibraltar" glasses, D.O.T.
French pressed-glass pitchers,
Bennington Pottery bowl; Pillivyut din-
ner plate and Chamblis "Vieux-Paris"
flatware courtesy Dean & DeLuca, New
York City.

Chicken Dinners

Sasaki's "Classico" wine glasses courtesy
Ad Hoc Softwares, New York City.
Plastic lacquerware "Tortoise" under-
plate courtesy Sasaki, Inc., New York
City. "Vigne" dinner plate, cotton nap-
kin, and iron candlesticks courtesy ABC
Carpet & Home, New York City.

Pasta Dinners

"Greenhorn" Irish linen picnic napkin,
green Terre d'Hautanboul bowl and
plates, "Almost Round" dinner plate,
and Kaj Franck carafes courtesy Ad Hoc
Softwares, New York City.

Pork Dinners

"Torgiano" dinner plate, cotton napkin,
and glass salt and pepper shakers courtesy Williams-Sonoma.

Seafood Dinners

Japanese "Peony" dinner plate and
"Boxwood" flatware courtesy
Takashimaya, New York City.

Soup Dinners

Leedsware tureen, silverplate "Baguette"
flatware, restaurant charger,
"Davenport" dinner plate, grapevine
napkin, and 14-inch paper doily courtesy Wolfman•Gold & Good Company,
New York City.

Vegetarian Dinners

Molin "White Crackle" underplate,
Japanese "swirl" plate, and linen napkin
courtesy Takashimaya, New York City.

SOURCES

INDEX

LEE BAILEY'S GOOD PARTIES

Favorite Food, Tableware, Kitchen Equipment, and More, to Make Entertaining a Breeze

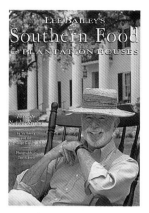

LEE BAILEY'S Southern Food & PLANTATION HOUSES

Favorite Natchez Recipes

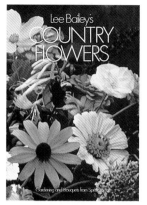

Lee Bailey's COUNTRY FLOWERS

Gardening and Bouquets from Spring to Fall

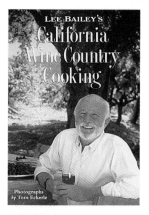

LEE BAILEY'S California Wine Country Cooking

Photographs by Tom Eckerle

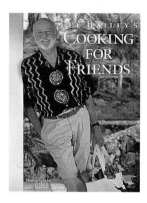

LEE BAILEY'S CITY FOOD

Recipes for Good Food and Easy Living

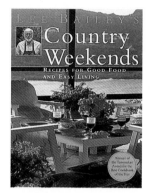

LEE BAILEY'S Country Weekends

RECIPES FOR GOOD FOOD AND EASY LIVING

> "Lee Bailey understands the head-long pace of modern life but never quite forgets the hunger for what was best of our past."
> —Food & Wine

LEE BAILEY'S Country Desserts

CAKES, COOKIES, ICE CREAMS, PIES, PUDDINGS & MORE

LEE BAILEY'S COOKING FOR FRIENDS

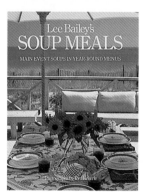

Lee Bailey's SOUP MEALS

MAIN EVENT SOUPS IN YEAR-ROUND MENUS

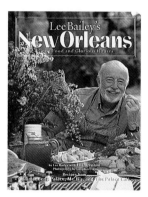

Lee Bailey's New Orleans

Good Food and Glorious Houses

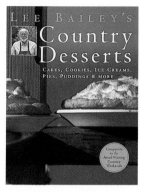

Lee Bailey's LONG WEEKENDS

RECIPES FOR GOOD FOOD AND EASY LIVING

Lee Bailey's TOMATOES

Photographs by Tom Eckerle

Lee Bailey's CORN

Photographs by Tom Eckerle

Lee Bailey's ONIONS

Photographs by Tom Eckerle

Lee Bailey's BERRIES

Photographs by Tom Eckerle